Contents

How to Use VALUE-ADDED ANALYSIS to Improve Student Learning

How to Use VALUE-ADDED ANALYSIS to Improve Student Learning

A Field Guide for School and District Leaders

Kate Kennedy
Mary Peters
Mike Thomas

Foreword by **Douglas B. Reeves**

CORWIN
A SAGE Company

CORWIN
A SAGE Company

FOR INFORMATION

Corwin
A SAGE Company
2455 Teller Road
Thousand Oaks, California 91320
(800) 233-9936
Fax: (800) 417-2466
www.corwin.com

SAGE Ltd.
1 Oliver's Yard
55 City Road
London EC1Y 1SP
United Kingdom

SAGE India Pvt. Ltd.
B 1/I 1 Mohan Cooperative Industrial Area
Mathura Road, New Delhi 110 044
India

SAGE Asia-Pacific Pte. Ltd.
33 Pekin Street #02-01
Far East Square
Singapore 048763

Acquisitions Editor: Debra Stollenwerk
Associate Editor: Desirée A. Bartlett
Editorial Assistant: Kimberly Greenberg
Production Editor: Melanie Birdsall
Copy Editor: Michelle Ponce
Typesetter: Hurix Systems Pvt. Ltd
Proofreader: Sally Jaskold
Indexer: Julia Petrakis
Cover Designer: Karine Hovsepian
Permissions Editor: Adele Hutchinson

Printed in the United States of America

Library of Congress Cataloging-in-Publication Data

Kennedy, Kate, 1979 May 3-
How to use value-added analysis to improve student learning : a field guide for school and district leaders / Kate Kennedy, Mary Peters, Mike Thomas ; foreword by Douglas B. Reeves.

p. cm.
Includes bibliographical references and index.

ISBN 978-1-4129-9633-4 (pbk.)

1. Effective teaching. I. Peters, Mary, 1956- II. Thomas, Mike, 1952- III. Title.

LB1025.3.K47 2012

371.102--dc23

2011033250

SUSTAINABLE FORESTRY INITIATIVE
Certified Chain of Custody
Promoting Sustainable Forestry
www.sfiprogram.org
SFI-01268

SFI label applies to text stock

11 12 13 14 15 10 9 8 7 6 5 4 3 2 1

List of Figures

Foreword

This helpful book comes at an important time for teachers and school administrators. While value-added analysis has been around for more than two decades, the widespread use of value-added assessment is just now exploding into common use. Moreover, there are many different forms of analysis using the moniker *value-added* that are widely variable in the assessments that they use, the analytical tools applied, and the manner in which they are used—and not used—for the evaluation of teachers and educational administrators. Even the best assessment and evaluation system is useless if teachers and school leaders do not use it to improve practice, and a commitment to practical utility at the classroom and school level is at the heart of this book.

Breaking Through the Maze of Complexity

The development of student assessments that are reliable and valuable requires the professional energies of test designers and psychometricians. Conducting value-added analysis can include mind-numbingly complex mathematics, such as variance-covariance matrices. But teachers and administrators need not become psychometricians or statisticians in order to apply the results of value-added analysis to the classroom. Just as we do not need to design and build the computers we use on a daily basis in order to apply them to our professional responsibilities, we do not need to design the analytical framework of assessments in order to use them.

From Blame to Analysis

While value-added analysis has been widely reported to demonstrate the profound impact that teaching quality has on student results, it has often been stuck in a tautology: The way to have higher scores is to be a better teacher; the way to be a better teacher is to have higher scores. But little has been established within the valued-added inquiry to identify specifically what practices differentiate the top teachers from the others. Indeed, when the research is stuck in percentile analysis, there will mathematically always be only 20% that are in the top quintile, and it is statically impossible for any more than a fifth of teachers to achieve that distinction. It is an unremarkable statement to contend that 49.9% of all teachers are below average in any place other than Lake Woebegone. Unfortunately, this sort of analysis, while perhaps interesting from a research standpoint, is unlikely to motivate any group of teachers and administrators I know. That is why Kennedy, Peters, and Thomas's work is so important. By placing the lens not merely on the data but on specific professional practices associated with gains in student performance, the entire conversation shifts from blame to analysis, from defensiveness to professional learning. The extensive quotations from teachers and administrators, including those with very strong unions, provide testimony to the fact that it is possible to use value-added analysis in a way that does not undermine respect for teachers or threaten a barrage of grievances and lawsuits if this tool is used correctly—to improve teaching and leadership. Importantly, the analysis includes all elements of the system, including factors at the classroom, building, and central office level that contribute to adding value for students. While teaching quality remains exceptionally significant, factors throughout the system can either nurture or undermine effective teaching, and this book wisely considers the entire system and its impact on teaching and learning.

From Micromanagement to Inquiry

Chapters 7 and 8 are particularly worthy of deep study and reflection. The strongest ideas this book contains are in the blueprint for a deliberate process of inquiry about the causes of learning and the nature of effective instruction. This is not an instructional system in which an external expert says, "I'm the doctor—take two of these and call me in the morning." Rather, the agendas, tools, and action steps guide staff members through a process of inquiry and discovery. That may strike some readers as tedious and frustrating. "Just tell us what to do!" they will shout in exasperation. But billions of dollars and decades of learning opportunities have been squandered by policymakers who insisted on giving teachers various recipes without giving them the time to understand what they were doing and why they were doing it. That is why implementation levels for even promising instructional interventions are low and the shelf life of most instructional innovations is typically only a few years. Years of initiative fatigue have led to a frantic game of Whack-A-Mole, in which policymakers simultaneously strike at every problem that raises its head, without ever dealing with any of them successfully. As Kennedy, Peters, and Thomas write, "Unfortunately, the result of trying to improve everything is that nothing much improves" (see page 48). When we shift the strategy from frantic to focused, teachers are able to focus on specific student needs and identifiable instructional practices, monitoring results and interventions in a clear and understandable manner.

Accountability as a Learning System: Five Warnings for Educational Leaders

As good as Kennedy, Peters, and Thomas's work is, I would not be doing my duty if I did not express some of the same concerns that the authors candidly acknowledge. Specifically, I offer five warnings for educational leaders and policymakers who intend to use value-added analysis. First, systems without professional learning are worse than valueless. Value-added systems will be and have been undermined when they have been used inappropriately. When teachers and administrators are drowning in data they do not understand, they will not use it to make better decisions. If teachers neither trust nor understand the assessment data, then a sense of despair and impotence creeps into a school that can take years to repair. In cash-strapped school systems and states there is a temptation to let the federal government fund value-added assessment systems but deny teachers the time and resources to use those systems wisely. Then inevitably, when the money runs out, critics will say, "See, we told you that spending more money on education was a waste." Buying a space shuttle without training the astronauts is an ill-advised strategy. Moreover, training is an endeavor that is continuous. A single orientation seminar in value-added techniques is not enough. Rather, data analysis must become "the way we do business," a habit, not a just another new initiative.

Second, accountability can be either a learning system or an instrument of brute force, but not both. Kennedy, Peters, and Thomas wisely suggest a focus on root causes and instructional quality. I might suggest that policymakers change the threat of "We're going to hold teachers accountable for their data!" to a more nuanced "We're going to hold teachers, administrators and policymakers accountable for their *response to the data*." I've worked throughout the world with teachers and administrators and have never met one that wanted to be unsuccessful, but I met many who did not know how to become successful. They will not acquire the knowledge needed for success with threats.

Third, the best value-added analysis will be undermined by tests that are not adequate for the task. For example, the vast majority of state assessments only have items associated with the standards for a single grade level, but the very nature of value-added analysis is that it helps teachers understand how students show growth when they are below, at, and above grade level. In order to fully realize the potential of value-added analysis, therefore, tests must be more frequent and include a broader range of items than is presently the case. Until states and districts fix this serious problem, schools and districts will need to have other measurements of students, particularly at high levels of performance, to avoid the patently ridiculous situation in which a teacher who has 100% of students meeting state standards and all scoring very well on state tests labeled as *ineffective* because there was no more room on the scale for those students to improve.

Fourth, the essence of value-added analysis relies upon making same-student comparisons. That is a far more reasonable assumption in stable suburban communities than in highly transient urban schools. Moreover, high poverty schools are also more likely to have higher rates of transiency as families move due to a range of factors including rent incentives, family disruption, and unemployment. It would be a horrible unintended consequence of value-added analysis for teachers to have an economic incentive to give more instructional attention to stable students than transient students. While some value-added systems address this challenge by using reasonable estimates for missing test scores, the process makes a coherent root cause analysis very difficult for teachers.

Fifth and finally, leaders must take care not to have value-added analysis supplant rational judgment. The daily work of teaching, assessing, and providing feedback to students remains at the heart of effective instruction. This daily work—planning and delivering effective instruction, intervening to meet the learning needs of students, and providing appropriate challenges and remediation where necessary—must also be the focus of educational leaders at every level. Value-added analysis can, as the authors suggest, inform the daily work in a powerful way. But the most sophisticated analysis will never replace the necessity for implementing and monitoring effective instructional practices.

—Douglas B. Reeves
Nahant, Massachusetts

Note: Dr. Reeves is the Founder of The Leadership and Learning Center (www.LeadandLearn.com). He is the author of more than thirty books on leadership and organizational effectiveness.

Preface

In the United States, we are in the midst of a painful transition from a manufacturing-based economy to a knowledge-based economy. Most of us know full well that the knowledge, skills, and dispositions that were required for the industrial era are different from those that are required by the new economy, but few of us seem ready to actually learn and do something different. The institution of education sits squarely in the middle of the storm. Our citizenry needs to be retooled, but the people who are largely responsible for this—educators—are also trying to figure out how to retool themselves. Given this conundrum, the most pressing questions for educators today may be, How do we get started?, How do we focus attention on improvement?, and How do we change the face of education so that the face of our economy can also change? These are complicated questions that require thoughtful, practical answers.

One potential answer comes in the form of a relatively recent innovation in education: value-added analysis. By conducting a robust statistical analysis of longitudinal test data it is now possible to reliably estimate the contribution of a district, a school, or even individual teachers on the academic gains of students. For the first time, many educators have a reasonably reliable measure of productivity. This sounds like a small thing, but it is not. Because productivity measures connect processes to outcomes, they are essential for any kind of deliberate systematic improvement. This is why value-added analysis is one of the best levers available to help educators move from where they are to where they want and need to be. But what is value-added analysis? How can it be used to influence educational improvement? How can it help educators to build on their strengths and address their areas of weakness? How can value-added analysis be used to help more teachers help more students?

This book has been written to answer these and other essential questions about value-added information. This is *not* a book about testing or statistical modeling. It is also not a book about whether value-added information should be used for teacher evaluation or for differentiated compensation. Instead this book is about *improving student learning*. It is a book written for educators and for those who work with educators to improve the quality of education that K–12 students so desperately need and deserve.

How This Book Is Unique

We wrote this book because, at this time, there is nothing like it available to educators. Much of the current discourse about value-added analysis is about the policy implications, the methodological concerns, or the evaluative uses of this tool. What has remained largely unexamined is the power of value-added information to inform and shape educational improvement. We believe in educators and in their capacity to transform themselves. We also believe that value-added information is the right tool to start the crucial conversations to make this happen.

This book gives us the opportunity to address the all too common gap between *having* value-added information and *using* value-added information (McCaffrey & Hamilton, 2007). Perhaps we can diminish the *knowing-doing* gap by first bringing clarity to what value-added analysis is and then by providing concrete guidance to use value-added analysis that is grounded in the real-life stories of educators who are actually doing this work. We used this approach because stories tend to be powerful educational tools (Rossiter, 2002).

Further, our intention is to help educators think about what they can do to improve the focus and the quality of all the learning that goes on in their building. In our work with educators across the country, we have experienced firsthand how value-added information can be used to improve both the breadth and the depth of student learning. We have seen educators transform their practice when they have had the opportunity to access, comprehend, and respond to their value-added information. We have seen schools turn their results upside down when leaders have instituted the mindset and the structures necessary to carefully examine and act on data. We have seen school districts boost their performance to unprecedented levels when value-added information has been thoughtfully and systematically inserted into the school improvement process. And in many places, student engagement increases, office referrals go down, and teacher self-efficacy skyrockets.

These stories are worth telling. They provide the impetus that most of us need to try something new and different. In this book you will meet Katie and Heather, teachers who used their value-added information to enrich the learning of all their students. You will be introduced to Kimi, a teacher leader whose school dramatically improved its results by carefully analyzing and responding to its value-added information. You will also hear about Tina and Bobby, principals who led their schools to remarkable levels of improvement.

Finally, and perhaps the most important reason we wrote this book, was to bring a fresh perspective on educational improvement. Improvement should not be an activity reserved solely for those who have poor performance evaluations. It should also not be an activity owned and led by outside experts. Instead, educational improvement must become a routine activity that defines what it means to be an educator. The good news is that ongoing educational improvement is not any more difficult than improvement in any other area of your life. It's about straightforward processes and continuous disciplined conversation and experimentation. It is about liberating and sharing the knowledge and the know-how that already exists in most schools. The value of data, and especially value-added data, is that it can help you identify and take advantage of the heretofore-undiscovered islands of excellence.

Whether value-added analysis is new to you or you are interested in putting your value-added information to better use, this book will help you think about and put in place the things you need to improve.

Overview of the Book

To provide a clear pathway for readers, we have organized this book around a common-sense, five-step improvement cycle shown in Figure P.1. Based on years of working with teachers and principals, we designed this cycle to be simple enough to provide meaningful support, yet complex enough to capture the real issues associated with improvement at the classroom, the building, and the district levels. The iterative process depicted below is not unlike other improvement cycles that have been employed in the education and business fields for years. Here we elaborate on the classic Plan-Do-Study-Act cycle that W. Edwards Deming put forth beginning in the1950s. The Value-Added Improvement Cycle consists of the following:

Step I: Jump Into Value-Added

Step II: Assess Results to Determine Strengths and Challenges

Step III: Identify Root Causes

Step IV: Produce an Improvement Plan

Step V: Take Action, Monitor, and Adjust

Figure P.1 Value-Added Improvement Cycle

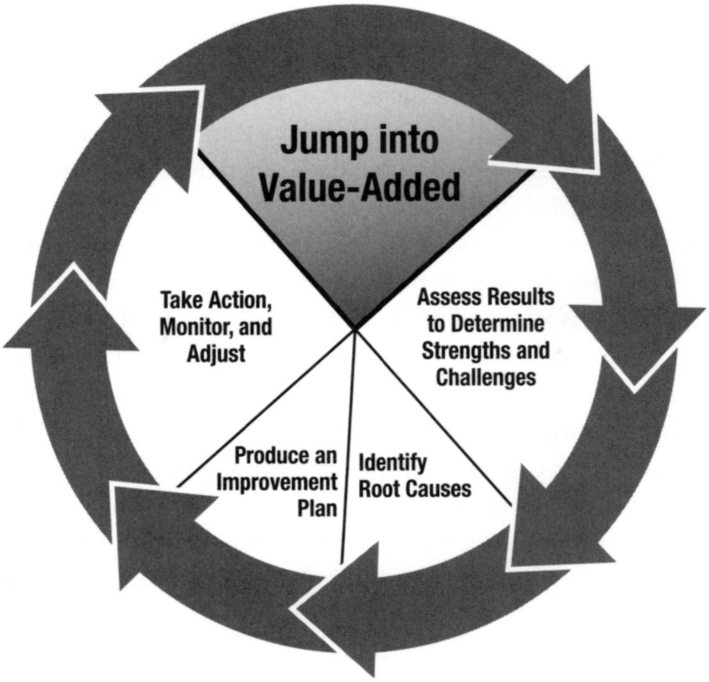
Jump into
Value-Added
Assess Results
to Determine
Strengths and
Challenges
Identify
Root Causes
Produce an
Improvement
Plan
Take Action,
Monitor, and
Adjust

Source: © 2011, Battelle for Kids.

Step I: Jump Into Value-Added

The first step of the cycle, Jump Into Value-Added, is covered in the first three chapters of the book. There is no magic formula for how to get started other than making a commitment to fully delve into it with purpose and zeal.

In Chapter 1, we begin by defining value-added analysis and differentiating it from achievement data. Making this distinction is critical to your understanding about how to interpret value-added results. It is also important that you come to appreciate the summative assessment role that value-analysis plays in a balanced assessment system. This chapter also addresses some of the implications of value-added analysis and points to some significant research findings that have emerged from this metric.

Chapter 2 focuses on how to develop the conditions for success with value-added analysis, including how to create a data-driven culture, provide effective professional development, and gain access to value-added reports. In this chapter you'll also learn how some of our school partners have jumped into their value-added reports.

This chapter includes practical tools to help you and your colleagues hit the ground running with value-added analysis.

In Chapter 3, the focus is on systemic educational improvement and how value-added analysis provides a unique starting point for improvement at the district, school, and classroom levels. We introduce you to our educational improvement framework that we call BFK·Focus. This framework takes the form of a multilevel nested funnel designed to take educators through a data-based goal-setting process. Through the course of this book, you will systematically advance through each of the three stages of the funnel at each level of your organization.

Step II: Assess Results to Determine Strengths and Challenges

Chapters 4, 5, and 6 engage you in the second step of the cycle—Assess Results and Determine Strengths and Challenges. In these chapters you will learn how to read district-, school-, and classroom-level value-added reports; produce a matrix to assess the results of those reports; and analyze disaggregated data to determine strengths and challenges of your district, schools, and classrooms.

Steps III and IV: Identify Root Causes and Produce an Improvement Plan

The third and fourth steps of the value-added improvement cycle—Identify Root Causes and Produce an Improvement Plan—are presented in Chapter 7. The primary purpose of this chapter is to describe a process for probing the root causes of your system's core strengths and most pressing challenges. Our intention is to lead you through a guided root cause analysis that results in a useful improvement plan.

Step V: Take Action, Monitor, and Adjust

Chapter 8 brings the value-added improvement cycle full circle. In this step, Take Action, Monitor, and Adjust, you will learn how to implement your improvement plan by acting on value-added information; monitor your implementation and make adjustments where needed; evaluate the success of your improvement plan; and then begin anew with fresh data. Along the way, we will share stories of teachers, schools, and districts that have moved from data to analysis to planning to action. These stories make clear that improvement is, in fact, a consequence of thoughtful leadership, systematic action, and continuous improvement.

Special Features

This book offers a unique, five-step, implementable approach to value-added analysis that will ensure a solid, robust plan based on your own specific strengths and challenges and inspired by the root causes of your own singular set of issues. Embedded in this approach is guidance on how to produce an improvement plan and then implement it, monitor, and adjust it as needed over time. Each chapter describes how to use the steps in the spirit of school improvement.

To support you in your implementation of the five-step process, we have included useful features in each chapter: case studies, real-life examples, end-of-chapter action steps, and reflective questions. The action steps and reflection questions will lead educators and professional learning communities in discussions about how to incorporate successful data analysis practices into their schools and classrooms.

A hands-on resource guide at the end of most chapters will include samples, protocols, and other tools to accompany the action steps for using value-added analysis. These will be short, one-page pieces that can be reproduced and used by teachers and leaders.

Suggestions for Using This Book

The learning-doing gap is a formidable obstacle that has stood in the way of many well-intentioned improvement initiatives. Perhaps this is because we have historically spent more time in the learning and not as much time in the *learning how to do*. Learning how to do is best when we can learn from and with others. Children do not learn language without others who encourage their speech and shape their verbalizations through modeling. Likewise, it is best to commit to weight loss by engaging in a program designed to teach us new behaviors and hold us accountable for measureable results. In that vein, we encourage you to engage a professional learning community to read and discuss this book with you. Together, the members of your community can not only learn about value-added information, but also make plans to put their learning into action. We recommend that one chapter be assigned each month to each member. Then, as a team, work through the discussion and reflection questions and action steps at the end of the chapters.

Putting Value-Added Reporting Into Context

By now you may be wondering where value-added analysis is available and whether you have access to this information. There are many places around the United States where value-added analyses are being produced, but districts that currently use value-added analysis to link student progress to classroom teachers are still ahead of the curve.

At this writing, sixteen states have value-added information available, and as a result of the Race to the Top (RttT) competition, there are many other districts interested in the possibilities that value-added analysis offers. States such as North Carolina, Ohio, Tennessee, and Pennsylvania provide value-added reports statewide. The System for Teacher and Student Advancement (TAP) partners with schools in 14 states and in Washington, D.C. and uses value-added analysis to support its approach to school improvement that involves multiple career paths, ongoing professional development, instructionally focused accountability, and performance-based compensation.

Several large cities also produce value-added reports. San Diego Unified School District and Eagle County Schools, Colorado, produce annual measures of student growth. The New York City Department of Education issues teacher data reports to show teachers how effective they are compared to other similar teachers across the district. Recently, the Los Angeles Unified School District began issuing value-added measures of teacher effects. Texas school districts—including the Houston Independent School District, Forth Worth Independent School District, and Longview School District—use value-added analysis to determine which teachers are eligible for additional compensation. As well, several recipients of federal Teacher Incentive Fund (TIF) awards also rely on value-added estimates to inform teacher award models.

Reform Initiatives

In a 2009 address to the National Conference of State Legislatures, Bill Gates, former Chairman of the Microsoft Corporation, shared his foundation's interest in identifying highly effective teachers. He observed that "when you see the power of the top quartile teachers, you naturally think: We should identify those teachers. We should reward them. We should retain them. We should make sure other teachers learn from them."

Gates's statement signals the high priority that the Bill and Melinda Gates Foundation has given to identifying, rewarding, retaining, and sharing the lessons of the most effective teachers. Its interests run parallel to reforms encouraged by the Obama administration. In 2009, President Barack Obama and Secretary of Education Arne Duncan announced the $4.3 billion RttT educational innovation fund. In order to compete for the funding, states needed to accelerate educational innovation and embrace bold improvement efforts. The RttT winners of 2010 include the District of Columbia, Delaware, Florida, Georgia, Hawaii, Maryland, Massachusetts, New York, North Carolina, Pennsylvania, Ohio, Tennessee, and Rhode Island. A key component involves teacher effectiveness and evaluation reform, and as such, connects directly to value-added analysis. RttT states are adopting student growth measures as one component of a multiple-measure evaluation design. Value-added analysis is a growth measure that links teacher practice to student growth and can potentially be used to identify and reward effective teachers and schools, as well as to inform teachers and principals on how they can improve their practices.

To give some idea of how value-added analysis has been put into action, we can look to the Benwood schools of Chattanooga, Tennessee. Once considered the worst in the state, Benwood, a collection of elementary schools, has achieved well-documented success by using professional development and strategic teacher placement and retention strategies to turn their school system around. "Benwood schools went from 53 percent of their 3rd graders scoring at the advanced or proficient level in reading on the Tennessee Comprehensive Assessment Program to 80% scoring at that level in 2007" (Haycock & Crawford, 2008).

What did they do to improve? Benwood principals and teachers began to routinely review value-added reports to determine areas of strength and challenge. Teachers observed and sought guidance from teachers who were strong in particular areas based on value-added results. The highest-performing teachers were recruited to teach the lowest-performing reading students in a privately funded after-school program. Those teachers and principals whose students grew more than expected received a monetary bonus. Throughout this book we provide other examples of how value-added information has been a centerpiece of school improvement. Your path to increased student achievement and overall school improvement can start right now as you begin to tailor these five steps to meet the needs of your own school setting.

Acknowledgments

First and foremost, we wish to thank the thousands of educators we've worked with over the years who have informed our work. There are many teachers and leaders we have talked with during the course of writing this book; a few we name, but many we do not. Thank you for everything you do to ensure students are learning *and* growing.

Jim Mahoney, Battelle for Kids's executive director, has been instrumental in setting forward a vision for using value-added analysis for school improvement purposes, and without his leadership, this book could not have been written. Every day we are privileged to work with many smart, mission-driven people who have been unwaveringly supportive of this endeavor. Special thanks to Mary Schultz, Joyce Ellis, Leanne Siegenthaler, Ania Striker, Rick Studer, Barb Leeper, Diane Stultz, Sandy Shedenhelm, Julianne Nichols, Leslie Damron, and Todd Hellman. Debbie Stollenwork, Desiree Bartlett, and Kim Greenberg at Corwin have been a delight to work with; thank you for making a momentous task as easy as it could be! We thank Ernie Morgan at the Value-Added Research Center for his insights and help connecting to New York City and Wisconsin value-added information.

This book relies on the hardworking teachers and leaders who took time out of their busy schedules to meet with us and share their stories. They are the real stars of this book. In no particular order, we thank Kimi Dodds, Tina Thomas-Manning, Bobby Moore, Heather Dzikiy, Susanne Lintz, Matthew Lutz, Melissa Krempansky, Mark Abrahamson, Amanda Garner, Renee Faenza, Lauren Collier, Alesha Quick, Revonda Johnson, Francis Rogers, Terri Stahl, Ned Kerstetter, Susanne King, Elisa Luna, Anne Lefler, Adam Withycombe, Maureen Tiller, Robert Tosh Corley, Nancy Shealy, Brenda Romines, Elizabeth Shindledecker, Jessica Cynkar, and Susie Bailey.

Publisher's Acknowledgments

Corwin would like to thank the following individuals for taking the time to provide their editorial insight and guidance:

Sherry L. Annee
Biotechnology Instructor
Brebeuf Jesuit Preparatory School
Indianapolis, IN

Dalane E. Bouillion
Associate Superintendent for Curriculum and Instructional Services
Spring ISD
Houston, TX

Barbara Smith Chalou
Professor
University of Maine at Presque Isle
Presque Isle, ME

Catherine Duffy
English Department Chairperson
Three Village Central School District
Stony Brook, NY

Kathy J. Grover
Assistant Superintendent
Clever Public Schools
Clever, MO

Martin J. Hudacs
Superintendent
Solanco School District
Quarryville, PA

Glen Ishiwata
Superintendent
Moreland School District
San Jose, CA

Dee Martindale
K–8 STEM Coordinator
Reynoldsburg City Schools
Reynoldsburg, OH

Patti Palmer
Sixth-Grade Teacher
Wynford Elementary School
Bucyrus, OH

Joy Rose
Retired High School Principal
Westerville South High School
Westerville, OH

Jill Shackelford
Superintendent
Kansas City Kansas Public Schools
Kansas City, KS

Janet Slowman-Chee
Special Education Director
Central Consolidated Schools
Shiprock, NM

Lyne Ssebikindu
Assistant Principal
Crump Elementary School
Memphis, TN

About the Authors

We are former teachers, education leaders, and researchers who work at Battelle for Kids—a national, not-for-profit organization that provides strategic counsel and innovative solutions for today's complex educational-improvement challenges.

Kate Kennedy helps teachers and leaders to better use and understand their value-added information. She also designs and leads professional learning experiences focused on formative instructional practices. Kate earned a master of education leadership from Teachers College, Columbia University, a master of arts in elementary education from Loyola Marymount University, and a bachelor of arts in women's studies from The Ohio State University. She is a former teacher and Teach For America corps member. Kate lives in Columbus, Ohio, with her husband, Matt, and young sons, Nathan and Owen.

Mary Peters has been a lifelong advocate for all children to have equitable opportunities to a high-quality education. Mary has worked at the classroom, district, college, and state levels. She is an expert on special education, data and value-added analysis and currently leads a state-wide rollout of value-added analysis in Ohio. Mary holds a PhD in education from The Ohio State University, a master of arts from University of Connecticut, and a bachelor of science from The State University of Geneseo, New York. She has developed and led several grant projects that pertain to teacher effectiveness. Mary and her husband, David, collectively have four children and live in Westerville, Ohio.

Mike Thomas has worked throughout his career to help educators improve their practice. As a part of this work, he has created tools, resources, and professional development experiences to help educators understand and use value-added analysis for improvement at the district, school, and individual teacher levels. Mike has also studied and presented all over the country on the topic of highly effective teachers. Mike holds a PhD in educational leadership from The Ohio State University, a master of science in future studies from the University of Houston, and a bachelor of science in physics from Otterbein College. Mike is happily married to his wife, Lu Anne, a proud father of three children, Lindsay, Christopher, and Emily, and a doting grandfather to Kameron.

1

Step I

What Is Value-Added Analysis?

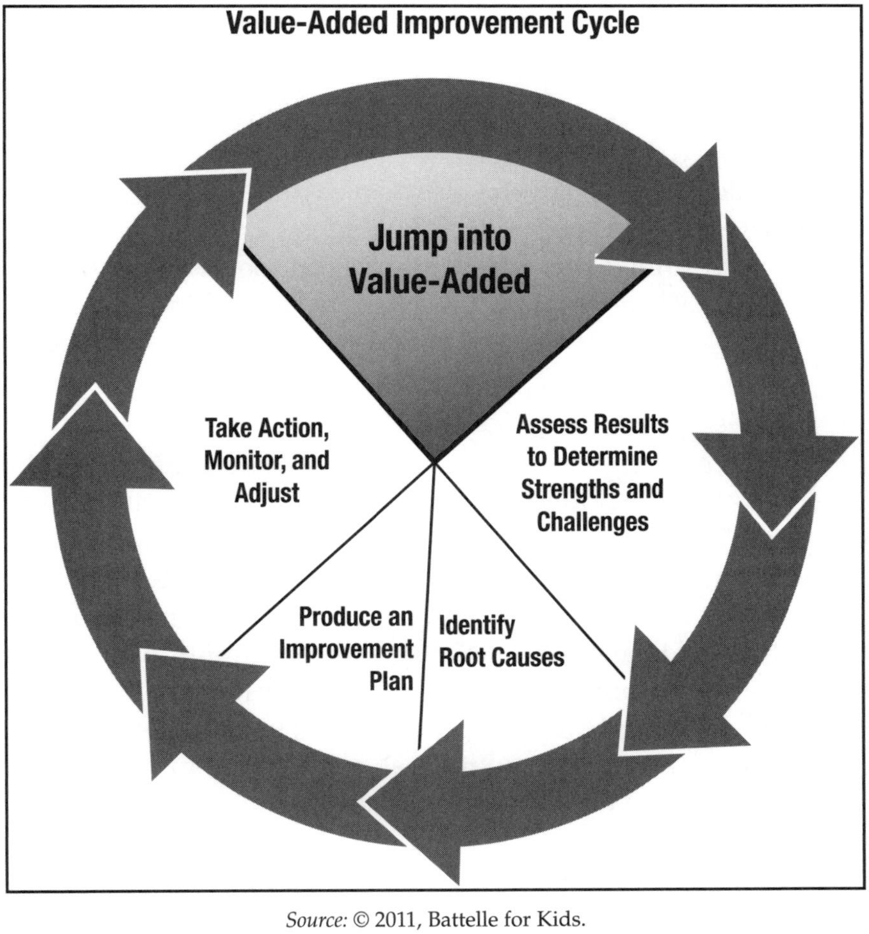
Value-Added Improvement Cycle
Jump into Value-Added
Assess Results to Determine Strengths and Challenges
Identify Root Causes
Produce an Improvement Plan
Take Action, Monitor, and Adjust

Source: © 2011, Battelle for Kids.

Chapter 1 Core Concepts

1. Definition of value-added analysis.
2. Socioeconomic status and achievement are correlated.
3. Value-added analysis: a fairer measure.
4. The power of two: progress and achievement.
5. Value-added analysis is part of a balanced assessment system.

Concept 1: Definition of Value-Added Analysis

What do educators say about value-added analysis? Here are a few of the many comments we've received from teachers and leaders over the years:

- "Value-added analysis is an extremely powerful tool for determining if we are effective or ineffective in our efforts to improve student learning."
- "Value-added analysis helps us recognize student growth and is a real agent for positive change."
- "Value-added analysis is truly a great tool for administrators and teachers to show if students are making appropriate gains. Teachers can really use this information to self-reflect on their teaching."

So what exactly is this tool that so many educators are finding useful? First, value-added is *not* a new concept, nor is it limited to education. The origin of the term *value-added* comes from economics and means the value that is added to raw materials through the processes of production. The term has since come to mean any output that is worth more than the sum of the inputs. Value-added marketing, for example, means creating excess demand for a particular product thereby driving up the price; value-added engineering refers to producing additional efficiencies in a particular process; and value-added legal services refers to "winning" legal strategies.

In an educational context, value-added analysis is a progress metric that estimates teachers', schools', and districts' impact on students' academic performances over time. Individual achievement data taken from statewide achievement tests are used to produce the analysis.

Value-added analysis is a progress metric that estimates teachers', schools', and districts' impact on students' academic performances over time.

In simplest terms, value-added is the difference between a student's baseline performance (prior years' tests) and his or her observed performance (this year's test). This can be compared with how a child's growth is monitored on a pediatrician's growth chart.

We know looking at student growth is not new to you. In fact, there are many ways to formally and informally measure student performance over time. As a teacher, one of the authors used classroom diagnostic tests to track student reading comprehension at the beginning, middle, and end of each school year. She charted her students' growth and used the information to set growth goals with students. Many leaders that we work with spend hours inputting state achievement scores into spreadsheets at the start of a new academic year to determine if students grew from one year to the next. These are simple ways of looking at student progress, and while helpful in some ways, they have limitations.

To be clear, value-added analysis is not simply the difference between one test and the next. Sophisticated statistical modeling is applied to produce growth metrics that are valid and reliable. In the last two decades, statisticians have developed complex statistical modeling techniques to determine academic growth. Many advances have helped make value-added information statistically robust today:

- Modern computing power that allows student achievement data to be crunched and analyzed
- Consistent testing cycles, allowing comparison from one year to the next
- Availability of student testing history and longitudinal databases that store student testing history
- Application of appropriate statistical tools and interactive data displays

As a result, value-added analysis has become a compelling means by which to depict and examine student progress. It represents a new approach for measuring the ways in which teaching affects learning and is a fairer and more reliable means of looking at student growth.

> Value-added analysis represents a new approach for measuring the ways in which teaching affects learning and is a fairer and more reliable means of looking at student growth.

This is an exciting advance from several perspectives. Educators can now access accurate information to identify not only the progress made by individual students but also the extent to which individual teachers, schools, and districts have contributed to that progress. Value-added information empowers educators to examine how well the education program they provide contributes to the academic growth of each student. From here, educators can determine how well their instructional programs are working, for whom their teaching strategies may be best suited, and where changes should be made. As well, teachers who create learning environments in which all students progress, regardless of their starting point, can be recognized for their success.

School districts that make value-added information available to their communities can provide evidence of school progress where in the past all that parents could see was the percentage of students passing high-stakes achievement tests. Some schools, despite failing to meet achievement standards, find they are contributing significantly to students' academic progress when they examine their value-added information. Data are not in short supply. Indeed, educators typically receive a plethora of achievement and survey data that are meant to elicit decisive and informed action. In some cases, educators report being unable to sift through a virtual sea of numbers to determine which of those data are most valuable to their school improvement efforts. A Tennessee principal remarked to us that "People who see value-added as just another data point are missing the boat." We agree and maintain that value-added analysis can provide information that is highly useful for administrators and teachers to efficiently uncover and prioritize areas of strength and challenge. Although no single form of information can be the solution for improving results, we are certain that value-added information deserves your time and attention.

Value-Added: Too Complicated for Educators?

Some think that value-added analysis is too complicated for educators to understand and therefore should not be used. Admittedly, the statistical methodologies that are used to create value-added estimates are, in fact, complex. However, we argue that the process of interpreting and using value-added information is *not* complex. Consider a few of the complex things we use and trust every day:

- *Digital watch.* You wear a watch and trust it to tell you what time it is, but you don't know how to build a digital watch (or at least we don't).
- *Actuary tables.* The tables used by insurance adjusters are a mystery to us, but we trust our insurance agents to charge us fairly for our insurance rates.
- *Hybrid car.* A Toyota Prius whispers along the highway getting 45 miles to the gallon. We love the impressive technology behind it, and we're glad for the fuel economy, but we don't understand how the Prius engine is constructed.

A Story of Two Students: Yanira and Ally

To illustrate a few points about value-added analysis, we share the stories of two students, Yanira and Ally. Yanira is a fifth-grade student in inner-city Los Angeles, California, at Alamos Elementary School, a school with 99% of its students living in poverty. In Yanira's classroom, California state achievement scores are low, ranging from the 4th to the 50th percentile. California requires that 75% of all students reach proficiency; in other words, all of the students in Yanira's class enter the door very far from proficient.

To the outside world, Yanira's classroom and school appear to be failures. After all, every student in her class is below the proficiency bar. However, Yanira's teacher works hard to raise student achievement levels and knows that she grew a tremendous amount in only one year. Classroom assessments revealed that Yanira started out the year reading at a second-grade level and ended the year at a fifth-grade reading level. That's three years' worth of progress in one year of schooling! At the end of the school year, however, Yanira scores in the 49th percentile on the state achievement test. Even though she started out in the 29th percentile, she still isn't proficient on the sixth-grade California achievement test. Yanira, her teachers, and her school would be considered failures in an accountability system where only passage rates matter.

Ally attends school on the other side of Los Angeles at Bethany Elementary School where 20% of its students are living in poverty. Fifth-grade students in Ally's class start out the year with state achievement scores ranging from the 50th to the 95th percentiles. Ally begins the year in the 88th percentile on the state achievement test and at the end of the year scores in the 80th percentile. Both scores are considered proficient. The school exceeded the state benchmark with 78% of students passing, but fell from 80% in the previous year. The teachers at this school work hard to raise or maintain student achievement levels. Even though Ally actually declined that school year, dropping from the 88th to the 80th percentil, she is still above the proficiency bar. Bethany Elementary School and Ally's teacher are viewed as successful.

AYP Growth Model

Another way to think about measuring growth is to project the *future growth* of students based on their individual history of performance. In the United States, as of 2005, *growth modeling* has served as an additional means to determine whether schools are making adequate yearly progress, or AYP.

Fifteen states have participated in a federal pilot project that uses growth modeling to satisfy AYP requirements, and all states have been invited to participate. The majority of the states are using a growth projection model, which helps schools meet AYP if their students are projected to be proficient in the future.

In Ohio, for example, many schools have benefited from the growth projection model. The growth measure is applied to each subgroup that fails to meet AYP after the "safe harbor" and two-year average provisions have been applied. At this point, the growth measure is used to calculate the percentage of students who are on track to meet the AYP standard. Each student with greater than a 50% probability of meeting the AYP standard in the future is considered to be on track. The future probability of meeting AYP standards is based on projections made two years into the future for schools that include Grades 4 through 8.

Concept 2: Socioeconomic Status and Achievement Are Correlated

There are classrooms like Yanira's and Ally's all over the country. Until recently, we have relied solely on achievement data to tell us whether classrooms, schools, and districts are teaching students what they need to know. What's wrong with looking only at achievement data? Let's look at Ohio's achievement data to answer this question.

The scatter plot in Figure 1.1 shows the relationship between socioeconomic status and achievement in the state of Ohio. Each point on the graph represents a school building. The schools are placed on the scatter plot according to their socioeconomic status (*x*-axis), as measured by federal free/reduced lunch numbers and achievement on the Ohio performance index (*y*-axis). What do you see? How are achievement and socioeconomic status related? Is there a strong or weak relationship?

The scatter plot demonstrates a strong relationship between achievement scores and socioeconomic status. In general, the higher the poverty levels are in a school, the lower the achievement scores tend to be. The reverse is also true: Less poverty in a school generally means there will be higher achievement scores. Naturally, there are exceptions, but overall, there is a strong relationship between socioeconomic status and achievement.

> There is a strong relationship between socioeconomic status and achievement.

Why does the relationship between socioeconomic status and achievement warrant a closer look? As was illustrated in the case of Yanira and Ally, and exemplified by the scatter plot in Figure 1.1, we know that where a student lives often determines how he/she will

Figure 1.1 Achievement and Socioeconomic Status

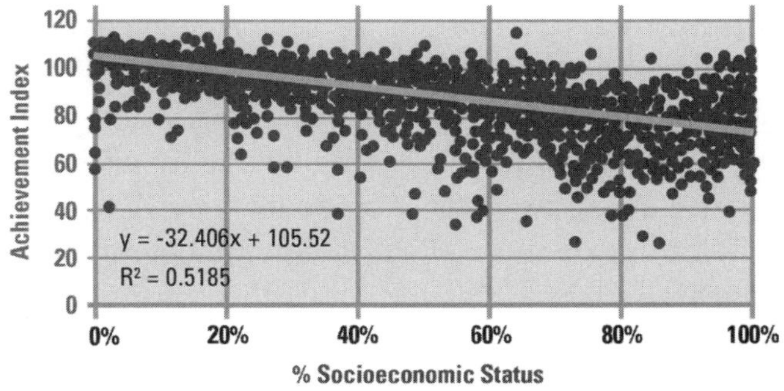
Achievement Index
120
100
80
60
40
20
0
y = -32.406x + 105.52
R² = 0.5185
0%
20%
40%
60%
80%
100%
% Socioeconomic Status

Source: Adapted from the Ohio Department of Education, 2009.

Figure 1.2 Ally and Yanira: Fifth-Grade Snapshot

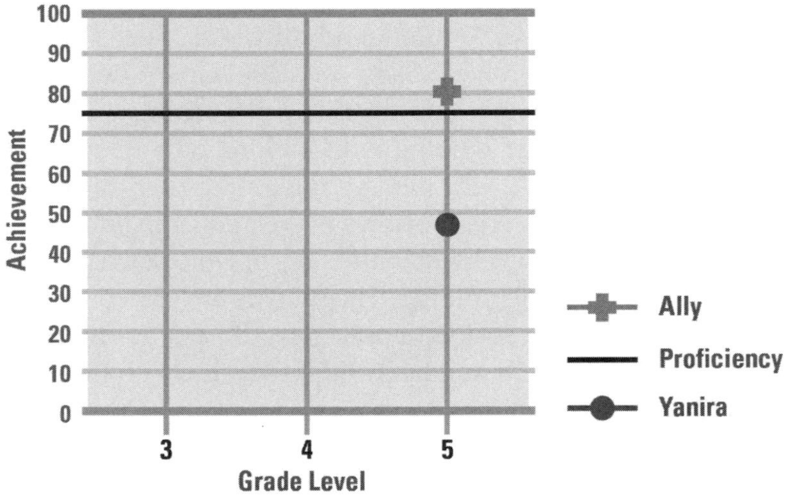
100
90
80
70
60
50
40
30
20
10
0
Achievement
3
4
5
Grade Level
Ally
Proficiency
Yanira

Source: © 2011, Battelle for Kids.

score on achievement tests. If we were to chart Yanira and Ally's fifth-grade achievement scores, it might look like Figure 1.2 (above).

This is how student achievement is generally viewed around the country: Ally is proficient; Yanira is not. We'll see a different perspective of these data later in this chapter. First, though, it is helpful to define achievement data and to examine the historically powerful role that achievement data have and continue to play in education.

Achievement data are a measure of student academic ability at a fixed point in time. In accordance with the No Child Left Behind Act (NCLB), each state must assess the achievement of its students in Grades 3 through 8 in reading and mathematics annually. Achievement test results tell educators what their students know and are able to do relative to the standards being assessed. Achievement results are reported to parents and the public each year. Often, achievement trends are displayed by presenting the results across multiple consecutive years. For example, the Grade 4 reading results for each of three years may show that the passing rates of students were 75%, 80%, and 82%, respectively. This information tells us about the overall reading performance of fourth graders across time for different groups of students, but what does it tell us about those same students across time?

Annual reporting of achievement results does not account for the differences among cohorts. Consequently, the achievement trend reports may be a comparison of apples, oranges, and pineapples.

Because each student cohort comes to a particular grade level with a different profile of knowledge and skills, achievement data are not particularly useful for assessing the quality of the current educational program. For example, a program may work really well for students who are on grade level but very poorly for students who have not mastered prior skills. So depending upon the profile of your current students, the same academic program may be termed either effective or ineffective based on the knowledge and skills of the entering group of students.

Achievement data have been around in various forms for decades. In most of the United States, this is the primary data source for school accountability. In other words, a school's impact on its students is measured by students' performance on high-stakes state achievement tests. The increased emphasis on accountability standards in the last decade has increased the emphasis on achievement scores. Schools are held accountable for student achievement through state reporting mechanisms and through federal AYP.

Achievement scores have value. They indicate the level to which a student can demonstrate mastery of information as defined by state-approved content standards. State achievement tests let students "show what they know," and higher scores can open the door to postsecondary work and college opportunities. There are, however, considerable downsides to measuring only achievement. The biggest downside—the most powerful factor in determining how well a student does on achievement tests—is socioeconomic status, as depicted in the scatter plot that we looked at earlier.

The landmark 1966 *Equality of Educational Opportunity Study*, authored by James S. Coleman, analyzed the achievement of 600,000 children at 4,000 schools. Reflecting on the impact of this research more than 30 years later, writer Hoff (1999) remarks, "Instead of proving that the quality of schools is the most important factor in a student's academic success—as its sponsors had expected—the report written by the sociologist James S. Coleman of Johns Hopkins University found that a child's family background and the school's socioeconomic makeup are the best predictors" (p. 33). The study, which came to be known as the Coleman Report, led to widespread public policy decisions based on the idea that socioeconomic factors contribute to student success, or lack of student success. Another important outcome of the Coleman Report is that some educators took the report to mean that what they do in their classrooms is inconsequential, for Coleman reported that background and socioeconomic factors are stronger predictors of success than the quality of schools.

Some teachers felt it was not their fault if students didn't learn, and these beliefs have continued to permeate our educational culture today. For that reason, the report is now "widely regarded as the most important education study of the 20th century" (Hoff, p. 33).

More than 30 years after the Coleman Report in 2002, NCLB was signed into law, turning up the heat on accountability for all. NCLB mandated that each state have academic content standards in place, if they didn't already, and that each child reach proficiency by 2014. NCLB raised the national awareness on the looming achievement gap, and although it is worthwhile to demand proficiency to academic content standards, NCLB has done little to emphasize the growth that is needed to help all students reach proficiency. Value-added analysis experts Dr. William Sanders and Dr. June Rivers (2009) have commented that NCLB's sole focus on achievement is "akin to winning the battle and losing the war" (p. 45). Researcher Ted Hershberg (2004) notes that "in its current form, NCLB is unlikely to lead to the necessary changes. . . . But if states adopt a new statistical methodology known as value-added assessment that isolates the impact of instruction on student learning, they will provide educators with powerful diagnostic data to improve teaching and put in place the necessary foundation to support a transformation of our schools" (p. 5).

So far, we have established that socioeconomic status is related to achievement and that a focus on proficiency alone does not account for the growth needed to reach proficiency. We have defined achievement and examined the powerful role that it has played in shaping our current accountability culture. Yet still, all over the country, classrooms such as Yanira's are labeled as failures. Another view of educator effectiveness, then, is worth our time and consideration: value-added analysis.

Concept 3: Value-Added Analysis: A Fairer Measure

Examine another scatter plot below. The graph in Figure 1.3 depicts the relationship between socioeconomic status and value-added gains. On the *y*-axis, zero represents no difference between where students score and where they were expected to score. In other words, a score along the zero line represents average or acceptable growth for one year. Negative value-added scores, or anything below a zero, represents less than expected progress. Positive value-added scores,

Figure 1.3 Progress and Socioeconomic Status

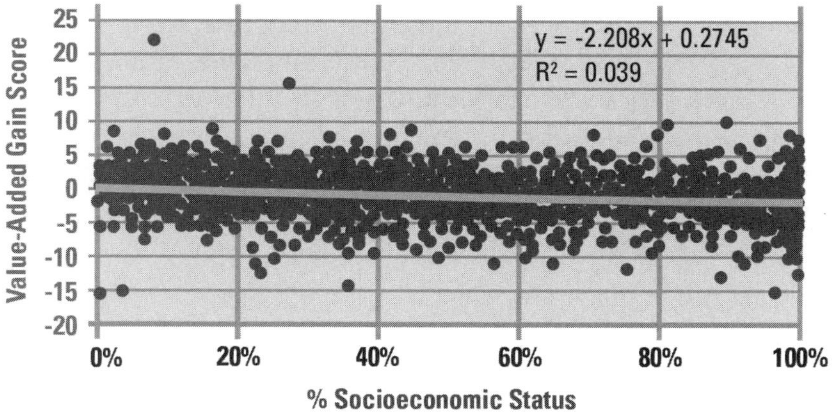
y = -2.208x + 0.2745
R² = 0.039
Value-Added Gain Score
25
20
15
10
5
0
-5
-10
-15
-20
0%
20%
40%
60%
80%
100%
% Socioeconomic Status

Source: Adapted from the Ohio Department of Education, 2009.

or anything above the zero, represent more than expected progress. What do you see? What is the relationship between progress and socioeconomic status?

It is evident from this scatter plot that there is only a slight relationship between value-added gains and socioeconomic status. In other words, students from poor families are as likely to have good value-added gains as students of wealthier families. There are some high-poverty schools that are making tremendous growth in one year as measured by value-added analysis and other high-poverty schools that are not. On the left side of the graph, you can see that there are some low-poverty schools that are making outstanding gains with their kids and others that are making less than expected progress in one year.

What conclusions can we draw, and what questions can we ask based on these charts? First, these graphs show that what we do as educators *matters*. We can't influence the financial circumstances of our students, but we can affect what happens with them once they arrive at school. Note that this is a distinct and important departure from the findings of the Coleman Report. Value-added analysis levels the playing field. Whereas achievement is correlated with socioeconomic status, value-added analysis has only a slight relationship to measures of socioeconomic status. This correlation was found by not only examining Ohio progress information but also by analyzing schools in Tennessee and on the East Coast of the United States (Hershberg, 2004). Therefore, it is safe to say that value-added analysis is a much fairer measure of what occurs in classrooms, schools, and school districts.

> Value-added analysis levels the playing field.

There are research and policy implications here as well. What are those high-progress schools, or those above the zero line, doing? Can we study their practices and replicate them in other places? What *isn't* working at the schools that are making less than expected progress in a year? Are there some practices that can be abandoned and replaced with more effective ones? Educators, researchers, and policymakers are using value-added information to begin to answer these questions.

Concept 4: The Power of Two: Progress and Achievement

Value-added analysis does not replace traditional measures of achievement; rather, it complements them. When taken together, achievement results and value-added information tell us where students are with respect to academic content standards and how effectively the current program is working to move all students toward higher levels of proficiency. We will show you how to identify patterns in value-added information—and what to do with them—in the forthcoming chapters.

> Value-added is the only measure that shows the impact that instructional practices have on student achievement.

Value-added analysis is an important data source because it tells you who is benefiting most from the current program—low achievers, average achievers, and/or high achievers. With value-added information, a team of educators may discover that the current sixth-grade math program works well for students who are at or above grade level but not well with students who are below proficiency. Given this information, educators can dig a little deeper into their practices and make a decision to change. They might add elements that make the program more effective with low achievers and/or abandon old practices that may not be effective. As one educator remarked, "Value-added is the only measure that shows the impact that instructional practices have on student achievement."

Value-added analysis provides a more complete, accurate picture of student growth from year to year, including how much growth a student or groups of students make over time. Together, achievement and progress information provide a powerful duo of measures to identify strengths and opportunities for improvement in schools. This combination is what we call "The Power of Two." (See Figure 1.4.) Achievement is measured by students' performance at a single point in time and how well those students perform against a standard. Progress, in contrast, is measured by how much gain or growth students make over time. To adequately gauge, encourage, and calibrate efforts, both progress and achievement must be measured and evaluated.

Each of these measures provides different and important information, but the combination of student achievement data and progress information is powerful. By measuring both and using other data sources, teachers, schools, and districts receive a more robust, comprehensive view of their impact on student learning.

Can value-added reports really tell us something that we can't get from achievement scores? Look at another example comparing Ally and Yanira (Figure 1.5). Ally consistently scores above the grade-level proficiency standard. She scores at the 96th percentile in math in third grade, the 88th percentile in fourth grade, and the 80th percentile in fifth grade. Despite being above the proficiency bar, her performance is declining. Earlier, when we only looked at Ally's performance in the fifth grade, she, her teacher, and her school appeared to be successful. How might they be perceived now? What intervention or enrichment strategies might Ally's teacher undertake if she had access to Ally's growth patterns over time?

Let's turn back to Yanira, who scores at the 13th percentile in math in third grade, the 27th percentile in fourth grade, and the 49th percentile in fifth grade. Yanira is making significant progress; however, she is still below the expected standard for her grade level. Although

Figure 1.4 The Power of Two

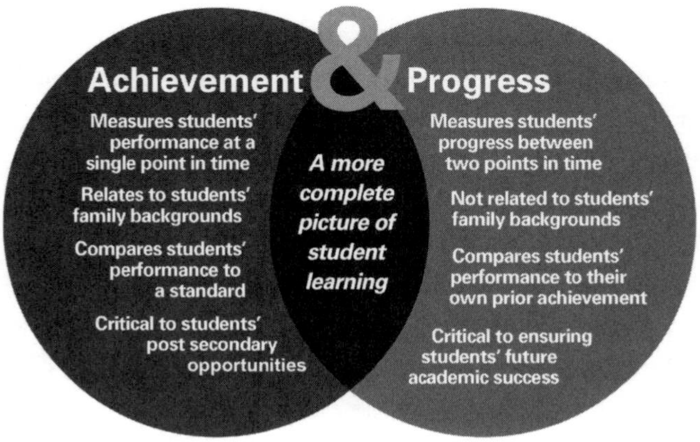
Achievement
&
Progress
Measures students' performance at a single point in time
Relates to students' family backgrounds
Compares students' performance to a standard
Critical to students' post secondary opportunities
A more complete picture of student learning
Measures students' progress between two points in time
Not related to students' family backgrounds
Compares students' performance to their own prior achievement
Critical to ensuring students' future academic success

Source: © 2011, Battelle for Kids.

Figure 1.5 Ally and Yanira: Growth Over Time

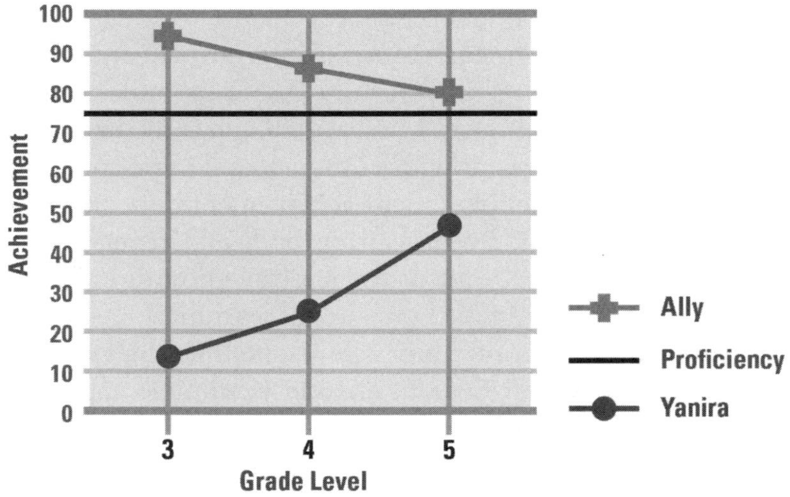
100
90
80
70
60
50
40
30
20
10
0
Achievement
3
4
5
Grade Level
Ally
Proficiency
Yanira

Source: © 2011, Battelle for Kids.

still below grade-level expectations, she is making gains. Before, Yanira seemed to be failing, but when we look at Yanira's growth pattern, we can see that she is actually growing at a fairly rapid rate. How might Yanira's teachers employ intervention and enrichment strategies if they had Yanira's growth information? How might the community perceive Yanira's school if they had access to more than just Yanira's and her peers' achievement information?

If we extrapolate Ally's and Yanira's achievement results to all the other students in their respective schools, our judgment might be that Ally, her teacher, and Bethany Elementary School should be rewarded. Conversely, Yanira, her teacher, and Alamos Elementary School should be labeled as failing and possibly sanctioned. However, when we consider progress, a different picture emerges. The success that Yanira's teachers and school have had in generating growth over time should be celebrated and shared, while interventions should be put in place to prevent Ally and students like her from continuing to make less-than-expected levels of progress.

Figure 1.6 depicts a framework that has been adapted from Dr. Douglas Reeves's *Leadership for Learning Framework* (Reeves, 2006). It takes into account both progress and achievement when looking at district- and school-level results.

This simple matrix juxtaposes achievement and progress measures to provide a clear picture of how schools or programs are really doing. When analyzing value-added and achievement data simultaneously,

Figure 1.6 Progress and Achievement Framework

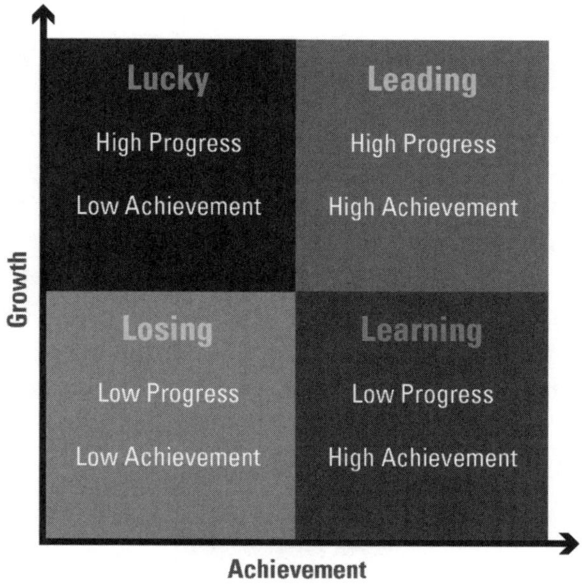
Lucky
High Progress
Low Achievement
Leading
High Progress
High Achievement
Losing
Low Progress
Low Achievement
Learning
Low Progress
High Achievement
Growth
Achievement

Source: Adapted from Doug Reeves's *Leadership for Learning Framework*, Copyright 2006.

you can quickly determine which cell schools may fall into on this matrix. Each cell represents an entirely different school environment. Is your school leading, learning, lucky, or losing? Why? In subsequent chapters we will expound on the use of a similar matrix to help you more clearly determine your systems' and schools' strengths and challenges.

Although it is important and necessary to hold all students to meeting proficiency standards, it is equally important for educators to ensure that all students—low- and high-achieving alike—are growing academically each year and maximizing their potential for growth. After all, our moral imperative as educators is to give all students access to curriculum and instruction designed to maximize learning no matter from which point they start.

Concept 5: Value-Added Analysis Is Part of a Balanced Assessment System

Value-added analysis plays a key role in a balanced assessment system in which both achievement *and* growth are measured and maximized.

In a typical school year, educators are provided access to some or all of the following pieces of information: state achievement test results, value-added information, common benchmark or quarterly assessment data, classroom summative assessment data, and classroom formative assessment information. Teachers and leaders are charged with the responsibility of sifting through and making sense of all of the available data to make reliable, actionable decisions to move students forward. Because it is a summative measure, value-added analysis is a useful tool to illuminate yearly strengths and areas of challenge.

Figure 1.7 depicts our schematic of a balanced assessment system. This shows a responsive teaching cycle where formative and summative measures are used over the school year to monitor student progress. The purpose of a balanced assessment system is to provide educators with the feedback they need in order to accelerate student

Figure 1.7 A Balanced Assessment Cycle

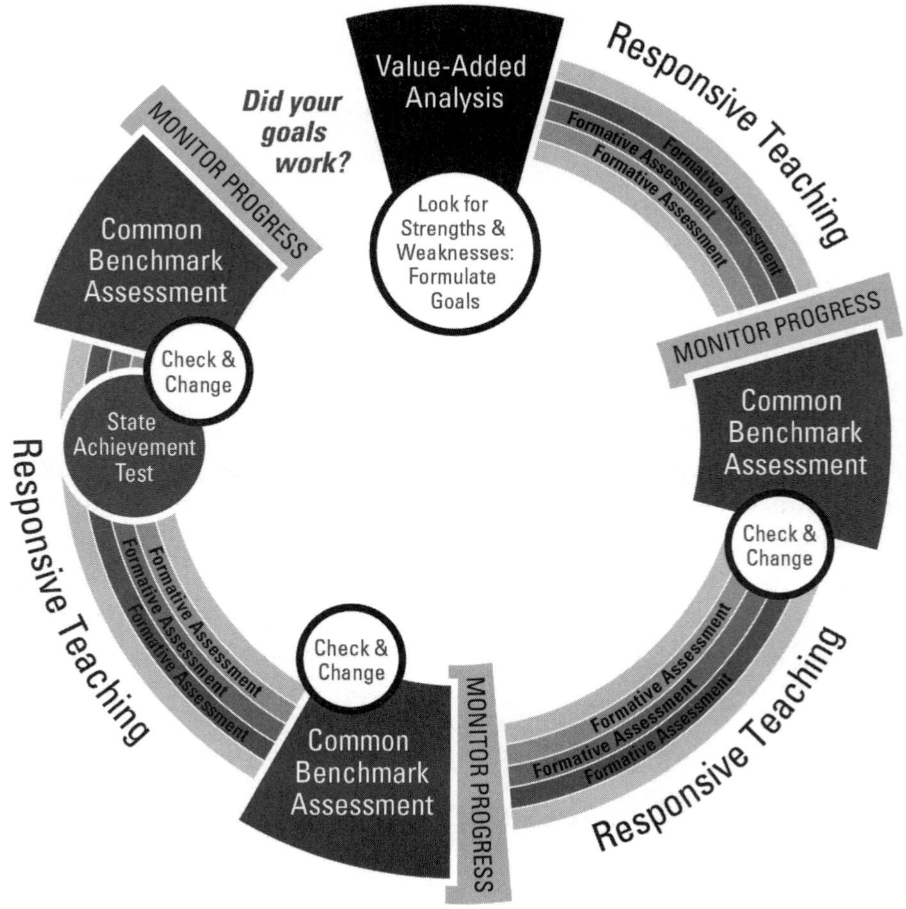
Value-Added Analysis
Look for Strengths & Weaknesses: Formulate Goals
Did your goals work?
Responsive Teaching
Formative Assessment
Formative Assessment
Formative Assessment
MONITOR PROGRESS
Common Benchmark Assessment
Check & Change
Responsive Teaching
Formative Assessment
Formative Assessment
Formative Assessment
MONITOR PROGRESS
Common Benchmark Assessment
Check & Change
Responsive Teaching
Formative Assessment
Formative Assessment
Formative Assessment
State Achievement Test
Check & Change
Common Benchmark Assessment
MONITOR PROGRESS

Source: © 2011, Battelle for Kids.

progress. In this model, educators are called upon to be responsive to the assessment information that they regularly collect to help them modify their instructional practices. In a balanced assessment system, formative and summative practices are necessary and complementary sources of information—to monitor progress in time and measure progress over time, respectively. We will further discuss this relationship in Chapter 8.

Concept 6: Teachers Matter

In direct contrast to what Coleman found in 1966, over two decades' worth of newer research using value-added analysis concludes that teachers account for the most influential factor on a student's achievement. In fact, Figure 1.8 shows that 65% of the variance in student progress can be directly attributed to the teacher, 5% of the variance in progress can be traced to the district, and 30% of the variance in a child's academic progress goes back to the school (Sanders, 2004).

Researchers have been highly interested in the impact teachers have on students and to what extent teacher effects persist over time. The University of Tennessee Value-Added Research and Assessment Center's Technical Report (1997) found that more than 80 scaled score points separated the most effective teachers from the least effective. In 2000, June Rivers followed students grouped by their achievement level on their fourth-grade achievement test and tracked their probability of passing a high school exam based on the sequence of teacher quality they experienced in fifth through eighth grades. Only

Figure 1.8 Teacher Effects Attributed to Student Learning

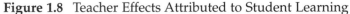

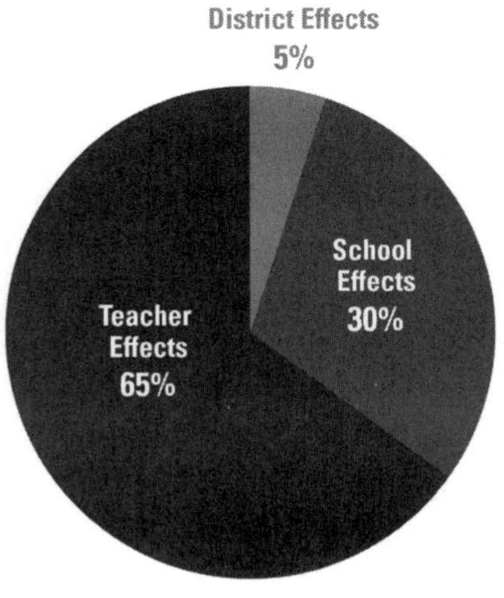
District Effects
5%
School
Effects
30%
Teacher
Effects
65%

Source: Sanders, 2004.

the highest achieving students at the fourth-grade level were able to overcome poor teaching in the fifth thorugh eighth grades and make high scores on the high school exam. Conversely, even the lowest achievers on the fourth-grade test were able to significantly raise their probability of passing the high school exam with a sequence of highly effective teachers, defined as those who facilitated greater than expected progress with students.

Dr. River's findings are consistent with those of Jordan, Mendro, and Weerasinghe (1997). In their study, children in a Dallas school assigned to three highly effective teachers in a row posted math achievement scores an average of 76 percentile points higher than their third-grade achievement scores, while those assigned to three less effective teachers in a row posted math achievement scores an average of 27 percentile points lower than their third-grade scores. In the research conducted in Boston Public Schools, students with the most effective math teachers demonstrated, on average, 14.6% annual gains in their math achievement scores while students experiencing the least effective teachers lost ground by 0.6%. In reading, students with the most effective teachers gained 5.6% in reading, while those with the least effective reading teachers made gains averaging only 0.3% (Boston Public Schools, 1998).

Writing about the impact of highly effective teachers, Marzano (2000) concluded that "exceptional performance on the part of teachers not only compensates for average performance at the school level, but even ineffective performance at the school level" (p. 81). And Rivkin, Hanushek, and Kain's (2001) findings suggest that having five years of good teachers in a row (one standard deviation above average, or at the 85th quality percentile) could overcome the average seventh-grade mathematics achievement gap between lower income kids (those eligible for free or reduced price lunch) and those from higher income families. Thus, high-quality teachers can make up for the typical deficits that we see in the preparation of kids from disadvantaged backgrounds.

When considering whether teachers have a lasting effect on students, Konstantopoulos (2007) found that teacher effects are cumulative and observed not only in the current or the following grade but that they endure up to three years in early elementary grades. Other studies have found, however, that the difference between being assigned an effective and ineffective teacher is largest in the short term (e.g., on end-of-year test scores) but tends to be more muted in the longer term (e.g., on test scores two years later; see, e.g., Jacob, Lefgren, & Sims, 2008; Kane & Staiger, 2008).

Clearly, the research base surrounding value-added analysis, particularly as it relates to teacher effects, has been growing. This is one of the reasons why educators, policymakers, researchers, and legislators are more focused on teacher quality. What is most significant is something you already know: Researchers have confirmed that what teachers do in the classroom with students *matters*.

> In this era of accountability and data-based decision making, we are reminded that progress is a crucial measure.

In this chapter, we defined value-added analysis in depth and clarified the difference between achievement and progress information. Together, achievement and progress information provide a powerful picture of district, school, and classroom effectiveness. Value-added information is meaningful and actionable. In this era of accountability and data-based decision making, we are reminded that progress is a crucial measure. In the next chapter, we focus on the multiple uses of value-added information and examine the benefits of using value-added analysis for superintendents, principals, teachers, students, parents, community members, legislators, and policymakers.

Summary

Value-added analysis is a progress metric that measures teachers', schools', and districts' impact on students' academic performances over time. Whereas there is a strong relationship between achievement and socioeconomic status, this is *not* true for value-added information. Achievement *and* growth should both be looked at to measure district, school, and classroom effectiveness. Research shows that what teachers do in the classroom accounts for the majority of variance relative to student growth.

Action Steps and Discussion Questions

Action Step: Understand what value-added analysis is and how it differs from achievement information.

- In your own words, how would you define value-added analysis?
- How does value-added analysis differ from achievement or attainment information?
- Why is looking *only* at student achievement problematic?

Action Step: Discuss the Power of Two with staff.

- What do we know about socioeconomic status and how it correlates to measures of achievement and progress? Why is this significant to our mission as educators?
- What new perspective does value-added information give educators?
- How can looking at both achievement and progress measures help educators?

Action Step: Examine the powerful body of research surrounding value-added information.

- What research finding on teacher effectiveness was new to you?
- Did the research confirm your beliefs or surprise you?

Hands-On Resource Guide for Teachers and Leaders

- The Power of Two blank graphic (Figure 1.9) for participants to fill in as they learn about value-added analysis

Figure 1.9 The Power of Two: Template

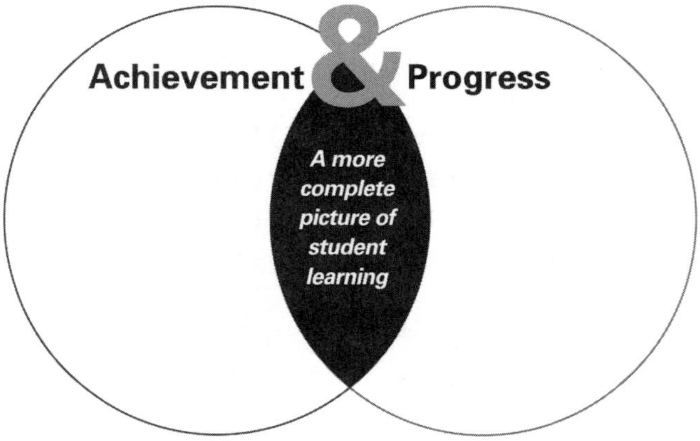
Achievement
&
Progress
A more complete picture of student learning

Source: © 2011, Battelle for Kids.

2

Step I

Jump Into Value-Added Analysis

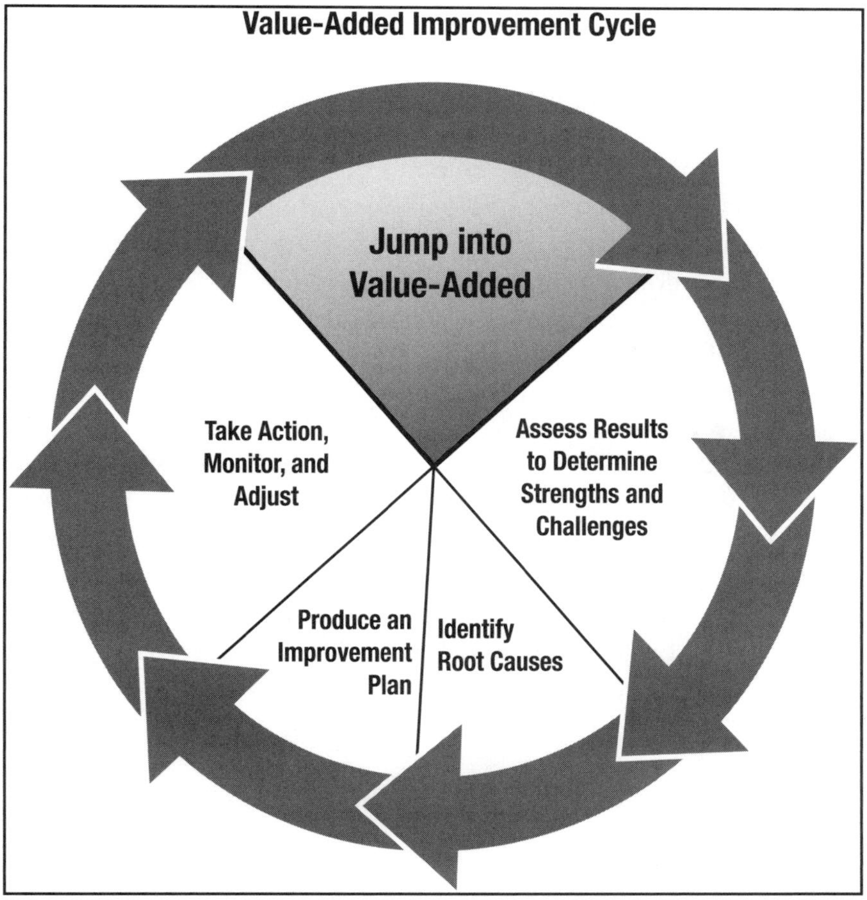
Value-Added Improvement Cycle
Jump into Value-Added
Assess Results to Determine Strengths and Challenges
Identify Root Causes
Produce an Improvement Plan
Take Action, Monitor, and Adjust

Source: © 2011, Battelle for Kids.

Chapter 2 Core Concepts

1. Develop a data-driven culture.
2. Provide effective professional development.
3. Provide access to value-added reports.
4. Equip educators to collaboratively explore value-added information.
5. Take a macro- to micro-level approach.

It's been said that a good beginning determines a good ending, and this is certainly the case with value-added analysis. In order to use this information effectively for school improvement, educators must be encouraged to jump into the information. *Jumping in* does not mean moving forward recklessly. Both value-added information and data-driven school improvement are new ideas to most educators, so to effectively use this kind of information, some careful planning, preparation, and training are necessary. The primary purpose of this chapter is to outline these preliminary steps and provide guidelines for

- Developing a data-driven culture,
- Providing effective professional development,
- Making sure educators have appropriate access to their value-added information,
- Equipping educators to systematically explore their value-added information, and
- Taking a macro-to-micro approach in the examination of data.

We will illustrate how educators, in various locations across the country, have jumped into value-added analysis at the state, district, school, and the individual teacher levels. Some of these stories are personal and some are more descriptive in nature, but all of them provide some insight into how to get started. We'll begin the first part of this journey by looking at the importance of developing a data-driven culture.

Concept 1: Develop a Data-Driven Culture

During the 2009–2010 school year, leaders in the Lubbock Independent School District in west Texas decided to invest in value-added analysis as a core component of the district's improvement plan. The new superintendent, Dr. Karen Garza, was already familiar with value-added analysis from her tenure as the chief academic officer in the Houston Independent School District. There, she was instrumental in designing a district improvement strategy that incorporated value-added analysis. Beyond a few district leaders, Lubbock educators knew little about value-added analysis or about data-driven school improvement, but at the end of two years of implementation, they are well on their way toward developing a culture that understands and makes productive use of value-added information. The question is, what did they do to get to where they are? In the next several pages we will talk about the important first steps that they and others have taken.

Get Committed

The first step in developing a data-driven culture is to make sure that district leaders understand and are committed to a particular course of action. This up-front planning and buy-in are absolutely necessary for success. As a part of this up-front work, there are two critical value-added considerations: (a) What are the intended uses of value-added information? (b) Who will be your value-added provider?

The Intended Uses of Value-Added Information

As a district, state, or other administrative unit begins a journey down the value-added path, it is imperative that leaders unequivocally answer certain questions: What are the intended uses of value-added information? Will it be used for school improvement; for research and policy development; for teacher evaluation; for differentiated compensation; for district-, school-, or classroom-level accountability; or for some combination of all of these uses? Regardless of the choice, each of these paths require thoughtful communication and training, but some of these paths have higher-stakes long-term consequences than others, and some of these paths have immediate consequences in terms of the choice of a value-added provider.

All else being equal, we would recommend that you begin value-added implementation with lower-stakes uses. There are two important reasons for this. First, high-stakes uses tend to trump lower-stakes uses. If people's first exposure to this metric is as a tool for differentiated compensation and/or evaluation—both high-stakes uses of value-added information—then these are likely the only uses that personnel will take seriously. Second, there is a learning curve associated with any kind of use of this metric. People need time, information, and experience to understand the strengths and limitations of this metric before they can trust it as a fair way to make judgments about their practice—and trust may be the most important aspect of long-term value-added usage.

The Choice of a Value-Added Provider

A second related decision is the choice of a value-added provider. There are currently several organizations across the United States that produce value-added analysis, but not all value-added models are created equal. For example, a value-added model that is inexpensive, simple, and works well for high-level accountability may not be appropriate for high-stakes teacher-level evaluation. A model that is robust enough to generate reliable information at the teacher level may be more complicated or more costly than district or state leaders deem reasonable. The key thing to keep in mind as you choose your provider is whether that provider can produce reliable information that serves the needs you have identified.

The intent of this book is not to critique the many value-added models that are currently available, but the choice of provider is still a critical decision. For some help in choosing a provider, you may want to reference a recent publication available through the Bill and Melinda Gates Foundation. It can be found at www.edgrowthmeasures.org.

Communicate, Communicate, Communicate

When district leaders have achieved the kind of clarity that is necessary for moving forward, the next step is to begin communicating decisions to all educational stakeholders. District leaders must be able to communicate in clear, simple language how value-added analysis will be used across the state, the district, or other administrative unit. When reaching out to stakeholders, leaders should

- Emphasize the importance of the larger improvement initiative.
- Illustrate how value-added information supports this agenda.
- Share with different stakeholder groups what will be expected of them.
- Assure stakeholders that value-added analysis is not a flavor of the month—it is here to stay.

Stakeholder communications should be delivered through multiple channels, including newsletters and other routine communication channels, and reinforced in face-to-face meetings. Principals and directors should take time in their staff meetings to explain how value-added analysis will be used across the district and within the different administrative structures. When meeting with teachers to discuss instruction and assessment, it is important to utilize value-added reports in conjunction with other formative and summative assessment data to show how this kind of information differs from and complements the information teachers are more accustomed to seeing.

It is important to utilize value-added reports in conjunction with other formative and summative assessment data to show how this kind of information differs from and complements the information teachers are more accustomed to seeing.

Beyond these initial messages, district and building leaders must demonstrate that they (a) understand the information, (b) value the information, and (c) visibly use the information in making important district- and building-level decisions. For example, are district leaders making reference to these data in their communications around core decisions? Do building leaders use these data to focus attention on particular building strengths and challenges?

When the Houston Independent School District (HISD) rolled out its Accelerating Student Progress, Increasing Results & Expectations (ASPIRE) educational improvement and performance management model—which included value-added analysis as a core component—district leaders used every viable means to communicate their intent: the district website, parent letters, newsletters, and staff in-services. The district also created an informational brochure for parents that explained the high-level goals of the ASPIRE model and included a simple definition of value-added analysis. An example of this parent brochure is included at the end of this chapter. These communications were intended to reach a broad audience, and they were repeated at every opportunity. For HISD, these messages were especially important because value-added analysis was going to be an integral component of the district's high-stakes decision making, including teacher retention and compensation.

The Ohio Department of Education invested resources in a regional support network to train educators statewide on both the accountability and school improvement uses of value-added analysis. This support network was put in place two years *before* value-added information was factored into the Ohio Department of Education's state accountability system.

An Important Note

Across the country, value-added analysis is increasingly being used for teacher evaluation and differentiated compensation. For example, some schools in North Carolina participate in the System for Teacher and Student Advancement Program (TAP) mentioned in the Preface. As a part of this program, schools use value-added analysis as one metric to compensate teachers differentially. Some schools, such as those in the Fort Worth Independent School District in Texas, participate in the Public Educators Accelerating Kids (PEAK) rewards model. In this program, teams of teachers are rewarded based on the gains their grade-level and/or subject-area teams produce over the course of the school year. Value-added analysis is also the primary metric in this system. Although the focus of this book is on using value-added analysis for school improvement purposes, it is obviously being used for high-stakes purposes. Whatever direction you and your district choose to take, we strongly urge you to develop a data-driven culture *before* you use value-added information for high-stakes decisions.

Creating a data-driven culture is a must when using value-added information for school improvement. Effective professional development is also a key driver in the successful implementation of value-added analysis.

We strongly urge you to develop a data-driven culture *before* you use value-added information for high-stakes decisions.

Concept 2: Provide Effective Professional Development

Kimi Dodds is a veteran classroom teacher at Blendon Middle School in Westerville, a large suburban school district outside of Columbus, Ohio. She gives value-added information "all the credit for our building turning things around at all levels." And turn things around they did. In 2004, almost every group of students at Blendon was making considerably less than expected progress in mathematics. In their most recent set of value-added reports every student subgroup, from low achievers to high achievers, was making more than expected gains. In addition, Blendon recently earned a school accountability rating of Excellent with Distinction, the top category in the Ohio educational accountability system. And the staff is still working on improving its practices.

How did this underperforming middle school become a stellar performer in four years' time? Its staff underwent a total transformation due in part to careful examination of their value-added information. Let's look more closely at Blendon's transformation story to analyze how they engineered this dramatic turnaround.

The school's transformation began with effective professional development. At the onset of Westerville's value-added journey, the district designated one of our authors, Mary Peters, then the district's data and assessment director, to be trained as a district value-added specialist (DVAS) through the Ohio Department of Education. Mary and others in DVAS positions across the state participated in five days of hands-on training on how to understand and make use of value-added reports. Following the training, Mary studied and shared value-added results with building leaders across her district. Over the course of this work, Mary became a district champion for value-added usage.

The steps taken in Westerville serve as a model for what other districts should consider:

1. Assign a person to act as the district's data expert.
2. Ensure that this person receives the training he or she needs to become value-added competent.
3. Allow the specialist ample time and space to help building leaders interpret and use their value-added reports.

In Lubbock, Texas, there were two levels of training. The district began by assembling a core value-added team, a group of thirty educators representing different administrative units across the district to serve as value-added specialists. This group underwent intensive, hands-on training led in part by coauthor Kate Kennedy. When district leaders assembled this team they invited, but did not require, invitees to serve as part of this team. This is an important distinction. Because these individuals chose to be on the core team, in addition to their regular district or building duties, they felt a sense of ownership and were excited about using value-added data to drive instructional decisions. Currently, core team members serve as the primary value-added contacts in the district. In this role, they help principals and teachers with questions, prepare value-added presentations, and receive ongoing professional development from an outside partner, Battelle for Kids.

Principals and assistant principals participated in the next level of training. During each of the one-hour, two-hour, and full-day workshops, school leaders were introduced to value-added analysis and its uses through hands-on, interactive activities. Learning targets for the workshops included

- Understanding their role in the rollout of value-added analysis
- Developing an introductory understanding of value-added analysis
- Interpreting the information available in value-added reports
- Exploring how value-added information can inform school improvement

Ultimately, until principals and other building-level leaders buy in to the idea of value-added information, it has little value for school improvement.

Once effective professional development has been provided to the core team and building leaders, the core team can train and support teachers and other staff members in how to use value-added information to inform school improvement.

Professional Development for Teachers

To make this information useful for teachers, it is important to begin with what they already know and understand—achievement data. They need to understand not only how progress and achievement data differ but also how they complement one another. Achievement data tell teachers what students know and are able to do, relative to state standards, while progress measures describe how well the current program is working to move students toward and beyond those same standards. Second, teachers need to understand how to access and interpret the value-added reports that are most essential to their practice. This means that teachers should be exposed to both the aggregate- and disaggregate-level value-added results associated with their grade level(s) and subject area(s). Finally, teachers need experience in what it means to *talk through their data*: (a) What do achievement and value-added data tell them about their team's strengths and challenges? (b) What about their practice is producing these results? (c) What can teachers do to take advantage of their strengths and address their challenges? A sample agenda for a two-hour session with teachers is included at the end of this chapter in the hands-on resource guide.

> Teachers need to understand how to access and interpret the value-added reports that are most essential to their practice.

Concept 3: Provide Access to Value-Added Reports

Because value-added information is ultimately about educator effectiveness, it should be handled with sensitivity. But this is no reason to withhold such crucial information from teachers and unfortunately, in many places, access is being withheld. Reasons cited include a lack of certainty about (a) what this information really means, (b) how value-added data can and should be used, and (c) who is responsible for providing guidelines for data access and use. One of the primary reasons we wrote this book was to help administrators remove some of these barriers. We hope that by guiding readers through the processes described in this book, more school leaders will feel comfortable providing appropriate access to this information.

Districts and schools that are committed to using value-added analysis for school improvement can take these steps to guarantee that teachers have access to and understand how to make effective use of value-added reports:

- Designate a value-added specialist for each school; this can be a curriculum coach, a lead teacher, or an administrator.
- If value-added reports are provided through an online system, ensure that every staff member has a login name and password.
- Schedule a time to sit down with the staff—or in some cases, each teacher—to share the appropriate value-added reports.
- Use staff meetings to demonstrate how to navigate through and interpret the available value-added reports.
- Distribute paper copies of value-added reports during a staff meeting and interpret them as a group.

Access precedes use. Once access has been provided, work with educators to collaboratively explore their value-added information.

Concept 4: Equip Educators to Collaboratively Explore Value-Added Information

The principal of Blendon Middle School, Tina Thomas-Manning, was interested in understanding and ultimately making wise use of her school's value-added reports. Mary Peters, her district's value-added specialist, taught her how to access and interpret the reports. After taking time to explore them, Tina concluded that this information was powerful. Her school's achievement scores were low, but her teachers believed that they were in fact making good progress with students. "They told me, 'We know we're growing kids,'" said Tina. So she set out to see if the data corroborated what her teachers believed. In most cases, it did not.

After spending considerable time with the reports, Tina believed it was important to allow her staff time to review and reflect upon their results. Jumping into the data with her staff, even though the information was a bit unfamiliar, allowed Tina and her staff to have critical, data-driven conversations. She did this by meeting with teacher teams during their regularly scheduled team meeting time. During each meeting, she shared the relevant value-added reports and helped teams interpret their data. Teams were then given time to discuss the implications of the value-added reports and evaluate their strengths as well as areas of challenge. By visiting with teams during regular team meeting time, Tina was able to meet with all teachers about their value-added results shortly after the data became available at the beginning of the school year.

Not all building and district leaders will feel comfortable sharing value-added information with their staff because this information is new and different. Typically they wonder, What if teachers ask questions I can't answer? What if they question their results? Keep in mind that the power of value-added analysis is its potential to trigger critical conversations about student learning. For this reason, we urge teachers and leaders to jump into their data and spend time having these sometimes uncomfortable but focused conversations on the relationship between adult practice and student learning. A relatively straightforward protocol for discussing value-added information is shared in Chapters 4, 5, and 6.

The power of value-added analysis is its potential to trigger critical conversations about student learning.

Heather Dzikiy, a teacher in the Dubois Area School District in western Pennsylvania, echoed many of the same sentiments. She recommends just *jumping in*—that value-added information is "a tool instead of something to worry about." At the beginning of the year, all teachers at Sykesville Elementary School in the Dubois Area School District are given time during their in-service day to examine their value-added information. This is not a formal meeting but rather something that principal Libby Shindledecker encourages her teachers to do. From Heather's point of view, value-added information is "one of those things where trying it really makes you better at it. I didn't understand it at first, but now I just get it. I can do some quick observations to figure out if I am where I need to be. That comes with time and practice." During professional development with other teachers, Heather summed up her journey with value-added analysis: "I'm able to follow [my practice] after the fact, to see if I went in the right direction. I feel better that I am doing something that's going to be helpful. There are other times that [my data] isn't as good as it could be, but at least I can be confident that I can make changes and see if they work. It gives me an excuse to change things."

After you've created a data-driven culture, provided effective professional development, and ensured that all of your staff members have an appropriate level of access to value-added information, make sure they have time and the protocols to dig through the data collaboratively. This could be a late-start Wednesday during which teachers are given time in the computer lab, or it could simply be setting an expectation that staff will spend time reviewing the reports before meeting in their professional learning communities to analyze the data. Other strategies for collaboratively exploring value-added information include utilizing staff meeting time to conduct a data walk, analyzing various reports in grade-level teams, or working with department heads to dedicate department meeting time to the collaborative analysis of value-added information.

In the next section, we'll discuss a macro- to micro-level approach for examining value-added information. We'll talk about what this looks like and why it's important to move from high-level data to lower-level data.

Concept 5: Take a Macro- to Micro-Level Approach

Working from the macro to the micro level, as educators did in Westerville, is a great approach because (a) each level of reporting provides a context for the next, lower level of reporting and (b) a macro-to-micro approach tends to de-personalize the data and better allow for focused, data-driven discussions. Value-added information can quickly become personal because it shows how well educators have been able to facilitate progress with students in their schools and in their classrooms. This can be both exciting and unsettling. To ensure that staff members feel comfortable when looking at value-added results, we recommend beginning with district-level value-added information before moving on to the more personal reports, which include school, grade-level, and teacher-level value-added reports.

An Important Note

In this section, we propose that educators take a macro-to-micro approach to data analysis. This does not imply a top-down hierarchical analysis of the data. We do not recommend that a district-level team complete its analysis of district-level data before giving building-level teams the go-ahead to examine their data. A macro-to-micro approach simply means that each team begins its analysis with aggregate-level data and then moves on to its disaggregate-level data. This concept is discussed in much greater detail in Chapter 3.

When presenting these data to your staff, it is a good idea to project images of reports on a screen or wall as well as provide teachers hard copies of the data. Sample reports and ideas about how to conduct these discussions are provided in Chapters 4, 5, and 6. There are, however, some important guidelines to keep in mind. We suggest that you always begin a data discussion with a conversation about strengths. There are two reasons for doing this. First, educators need to spend more time talking about and celebrating successes. These conversations bring to light strategies that work and approaches that should be replicated. A second reason to begin with strengths is that a strengths-based conversation prepares educators to talk about areas of challenge.

> Always begin a data discussion with a conversation about strengths.

Questions to ask when reviewing value-added reports with staff:

- What are our strengths as a district? In what subjects and grade levels did we produce more than expected growth with students?
    - What is special or different about how these subject areas are taught?
    - Are there ways to leverage these strengths by utilizing some of the same strategies in other areas?
- What are our areas of challenge as a district? In what subjects and grade levels did we produce less than expected growth?
    - What is different about how these subjects are taught?
    - Are there straightforward ways to improve progress in these subject areas?

It is important to give your staff time to discuss these questions in small groups before moving on to school-specific or teacher-specific reports.

In Chapter 3, we discuss a relatively simple school improvement model that grounds this work. Then, in Chapters 4 through 6, we share more information about how to interpret reports at the district, building, classroom, and individual teacher levels, along with questions to consider when reading the reports.

Summary

When using value-added information it is important to create a data-driven culture. Superintendents and principals should be clear and up front about the intended uses of value-added information and how value-added information will be used for school improvement. This information should be shared with teachers and leaders in as many venues and contexts as possible. Educators must also be provided thoughtful and timely professional development about the appropriate uses of value-added information. Introductory workshops should focus on how progress and achievement measures differ and how value-added analysis can be used for school improvement. This book can and should be used as a launching pad for these conversations at both the school and district levels.

Once everyone understands what value-added analysis is and what it will be used for, teachers and leaders need clear directions on how to access and interpret their value-added reports. Access leads to use, which in turn leads to school improvement. Once educators have access, make sure they are provided the tools they need to collaboratively explore this new kind of information. Finally, when sharing value-added information with staff, leaders should take a macro- to micro-level approach. That is, start by discussing high-level district results before moving on to the school-, grade-, and individual teacher-level results. Going from the macro to the micro level helps educators put value-added information in perspective and allows multiple levels of success and challenge to emerge.

Action Steps and Reflection Questions

Action Step: Craft and deliver a clear message for how value-added analysis will be used in your school district with leaders, teachers, parents, and community members.

- How is value-added analysis used (or will be used) in your school or district? Is the focus on accountability or school improvement?
- How will you share The Power of Two with parents, teachers, students, and other stakeholders in your district?
- Have you incorporated information on value-added analysis into all of your communications, including e-mail blasts, website information, and brochures on district improvement initiatives?
- Do all key leaders in your district understand what value-added analysis is and how looking at progress information can provide a clearer picture of student learning?

Action Step: Create a professional development plan to help educators understand, interpret, and use value-added information.

- How will you introduce value-added analysis to your staff?
- Have you identified a core team of district and building leaders to serve as your data experts?
- Have you set aside enough time to make sure all teachers and leaders understand what value-added analysis is and how they can use it for school improvement?
- How can you build value-added analysis into the professional development structures that already exist in your school or district?

Action Step: Ensure that educators have easy access to value-added reports.

- Do staff members have hard copies of paper reports or access to their value-added reports online?
- Who in your school building or district would make a good data guru?
- What barriers to data access currently exist, and what can you do to mitigate these barriers?

Action Step: Set aside at least two hours in the fall for educators to explore their value-added reports.

- In what ways can you encourage educators to explore their value-added reports?
- How can you leverage staff meeting time, late-start days, or other professional development time to provide educators time to explore their value-added reports?

Action Step: Prepare a presentation that walks educators through your district's value-added reports from the macro to the micro level.

- What strengths do your district data reveal?
- How might you begin your presentation by celebrating successes?
- As you explore your data from the macro to the micro level, what questions and concerns do you anticipate?

Hands-On Resource Guide

- Introduction to Value-Added Analysis: Two-Hour Professional Development Workshop Agenda (see Figure 2.1)—Sample staff meeting agenda for value-added analysis overview
- Accelerating Student Progress, Increasing Results and Expectations: A Guide for Parents and Our Community—Houston Independent School District's ASPIRE communications brochure for parents and community members (see Figure 2.2)

Figure 2.1 Introduction to Value-Added Analysis: Two-Hour Professional Development Workshop Agenda

I. Welcome and Introductions

- District message about value-added analysis
- Context for using value-added analysis
- Icebreaker activity

II. Staff Roles and Responsibilities With Value-Added Analysis

- Understand their data
- Use data to reflect on results and make instructional decisions to make decisions
- Appreciate, collaborate, and inquire

III. Hopes and Fears

- Ask staff members to share hopes and fears about value-added information

IV. Introduction to Value-Added Analysis

- In small groups, discuss the differences between progress and achievement data
- Create working definitions of value-added analysis
- An Introduction to Value-Added Progress Measures DVD
- Revisit definitions and clarify questions and misconceptions

V. Value-Added Overview: What Do Value-Added Reports Look Like?

- PowerPoint on using sample reports
- Facilitate discussion on common patterns found in value-added reports

VI. Next Steps

- Share navigation and access tips with staff members
- Repeat district message on the use of value-added analysis
- Share plans and dates for other upcoming workshops and discussions on value-added information
- Set expectation that following this workshop, staff members should access their own reports and prepare to discuss schoolwide and grade-level results in professional learning communities

Figure 2.2 A Guide for Parents and Our Community: Houston Independent School District's ASPIRE Communications Brochure for Parents and Community Members

ASPIRE

Accelerating Student Progress and Increasing Results & Expectations at HISD

A Guide for Parents & Our Community

The Houston Independent School District is committed to providing all of our students a quality education that prepares them to graduate ready for college and their careers. In 2007, the district created a model called **ASPIRE** that helps the district align its educational programs, resources, and services to better meet students' needs and increase their academic progress and achievement. ASPIRE stands for *Accelerating Student Progress. Increasing Results & Expectations.*

ASPIRE:

- Connects all of HISD's efforts to improve the quality of education for children
- Encourages teacher and school partnerships to address challenges and share best practices
- Provides parents with information about the success of their child's school
- Recognizes and celebrates great teaching measured by students' progress

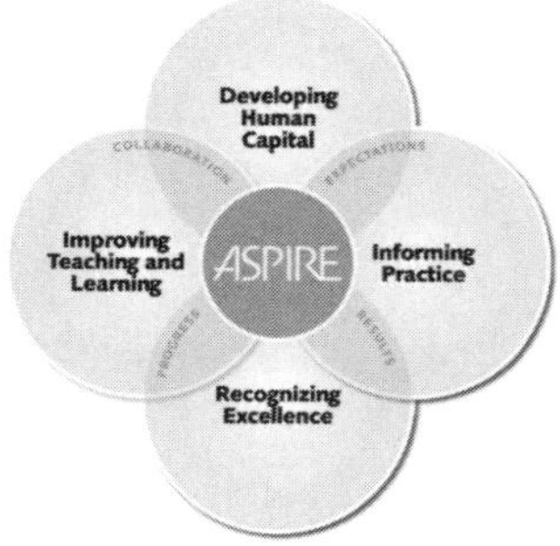
Developing Human Capital
Improving Teaching and Learning
ASPIRE
Informing Practice
Recognizing Excellence

An important part of ASPIRE involves using high-quality information, such as value-added analysis, to make decisions about teaching and student learning.

What is Value-Added Analysis?
Value-added analysis provides information that allows us to measure the impact that HISD schools and teachers have on students' academic progress from year to year.

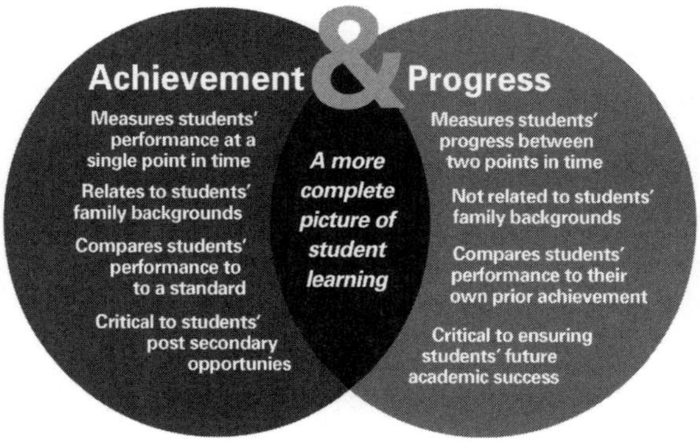
Achievement & Progress
Measures students' performance at a single point in time
Relates to students' family backgrounds
Compares students' performance to to a standard
Critical to students' post secondary opportunities
A more complete picture of student learning
Measures students' progress between two points in time
Not related to students' family backgrounds
Compares students' performance to their own prior achievement
Critical to ensuring students' future academic success

A More Complete Picture of Student Learning
When achievement and progress data are used together, parents, teachers, and administrators have a more complete picture of student learning and can better meet all students' individual learning needs.

www.houstonisd.org/ASPIRE

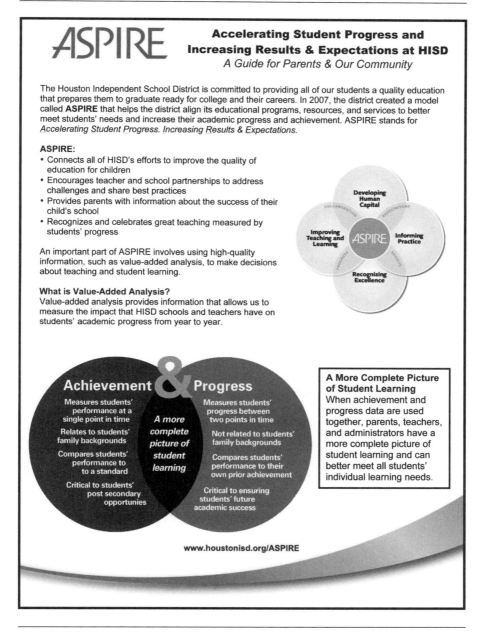

Source: Used with permission from Houston Independent School District.

3

Step I

A Framework for Systemic Improvement

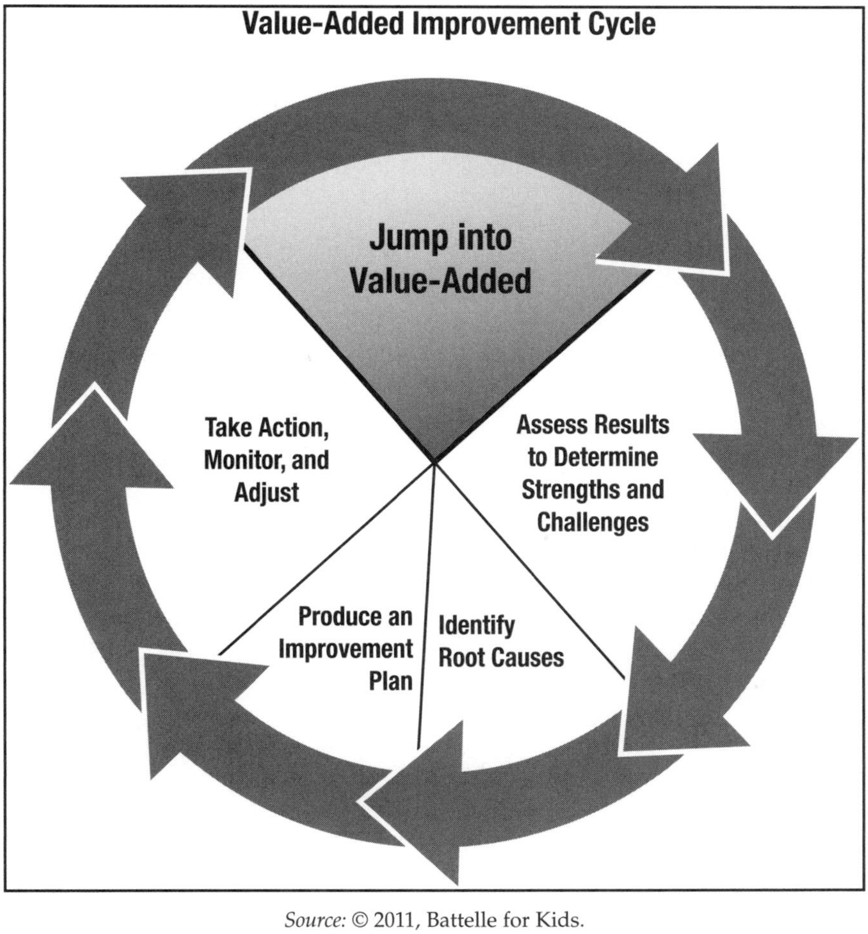
Value-Added Improvement Cycle
Jump into Value-Added
Assess Results to Determine Strengths and Challenges
Identify Root Causes
Produce an Improvement Plan
Take Action, Monitor, and Adjust

Source: © 2011, Battelle for Kids.

Chapter 3 Core Concepts

1. The meaning of *systemic educational improvement* has changed over time.
2. Value-added analysis is about program effectiveness.
3. The district, school, and classroom levels are interdependent nested systems.
4. Objective information is key to understanding the current state of the system.
5. Focus on the System—connecting levels of analysis and stages of inquiry.
6. The importance of Focus on the System.

Overview: Moving Toward a Framework for Systemic Educational Improvement

The primary purpose of this chapter is to introduce the educational improvement framework that serves as the backbone for the rest of this book. This framework, what we call BFK·Focus, is grounded in a set of beliefs that are derived primarily from the systems and organizational change literature and from the experiences we have had with people we have worked with. As you move through this chapter, you may find that some of these beliefs are counterintuitive, so it is important to take a critical look at what is presented here. Not surprisingly, some of our beliefs have to do with the connections between information and educational improvement, not to mention the special role that value-added information plays in our beliefs about systemic educational improvement.

This chapter begins with a discussion of the phrase *systemic educational improvement* and how the meaning of this phrase has changed over time. Following that, we examine how current structures at the district, the school, and the classroom levels tend to militate against the kinds of improvement that all of us desire. We then argue that systemic improvement is possible, and maybe even likely, if each level of the system responds appropriately to the data that are most relevant to their level of the operation. Finally, we examine a framework of three questions that allow educators at each level of the system to *work together* by working *independently* on the data that are most relevant for them.

It is our hope that by the end of this chapter, readers will understand the big picture of how value-added information fits into a larger discussion of educational improvement. Chapters 4, 5, and 6 are dedicated to looking in depth at the value-added reports that are critical for district-level, school-level, and teacher-level analysis, respectively. But before we get into these beliefs, let's bring some meaning to the phrase *systemic educational improvement.*

Concept 1: The Meaning of Systemic Educational Improvement Has Changed Over Time

Systemic educational improvement is not a new idea, but the substance and focus of systemic improvement have changed dramatically over time. For example, in 1957, the Soviet Union grabbed the attention of the world by launching Sputnik, the first artificial earth-orbiting satellite. This single event startled the United States out of its postwar euphoria and demonstrated unequivocally that we were behind the Soviet Union in the race for space. One of the major consequences of this event was a far-reaching critique of the U.S. educational system. In short, students in the United States were not being exposed to the kinds of math and science instruction that were necessary for the United States to compete successfully against the Soviets. The focus of the systemic improvement in this era was predominantly on more rigorous math and science curricula.

Two and a half decades later, in 1983, the National Commission on Excellence in Education issued another scathing critique of K–12 education titled *A Nation at Risk.* This report warned that "the educational foundations of our society are presently being eroded by a rising tide of mediocrity that threatens our very future as a Nation and a people" (p. 1). The report concluded, among other things, that the American educational system had to raise expectations, strengthen the curriculum, improve the teaching force, and lengthen the school year. The now common backdrop of standards and high-stakes testing in the United States can largely be traced back to this report and the movement it spawned.

Today, the primary focus of educational improvement is *teacher quality*. Like earlier demands for systemic improvement, this was triggered by the emergence of something new. Once standards and high-stakes testing became the norm across the United States, it became possible to conduct rigorous comparative analyses of testing results across schools, districts, and states. Initially, these comparisons were of little use because most of the variance in results could be attributed to socioeconomic factors. Students in privileged circumstances almost always outperformed students in less privileged circumstances.

> Today, the primary focus of educational improvement is teacher quality.

The emergence of value-added metrics largely solved this problem because value-added analysis compares the *gains* students make from one year to the next rather than simply comparing their raw achievement levels. With this kind of analysis it became possible to link student gains to the quality of their educational experience rather than just their family background. This enabled much more meaningful comparisons across states, across districts, across schools, and even across individual classrooms. The primary finding across all of these analyses was the centrality of *teacher quality* as a core variable associated with the academic growth of students. The enormous differences in student growth from one classroom to the next far outweigh any differences that can be attributed to school, district, or state influences. Hence the current focus on teacher quality.

So now, when policymakers and other interested stakeholders talk about systemic educational improvement, they are primarily talking about improving the quality, that is, productivity of teachers. As we begin to think about how this is possible it is important to understand the kind of information provided by value-added analysis.

Concept 2: Value-Added Analysis Is About Program Effectiveness

What do educators think about when they hear the phrase *data usage*? How about *data-driven instruction* or *using data to inform teaching and learning*? Twenty-five years ago, before the advent of high-stakes testing and state and federal accountability systems, there was almost no talk of data-driven improvement, because there were virtually no common data upon which to base improvement. Today, teachers often use these phrases, but like everything else associated with education, the meaning of data-driven improvement is still evolving.

For most educators, the phrase *data-driven improvement* refers to a particular kind of data usage—*item* and/or *strand analysis* associated with their state's high-stakes tests. As its name implies, this particular kind of analysis is aimed at helping teachers understand how their students performed on particular questions and strands of questions within the test.

For example, a particular fifth-grade math teacher might use an item or strand analysis to learn that her students did very well with *operations* but not so well with *patterns and functions*. Unfortunately, this by itself does not tell that teacher very much about the quality of her instruction in these areas. It could be that she actually did a poor job teaching *operations* but that her students already knew this information from prior teachers. It could also mean that she did a decent job teaching patterns and functions, but because her students had virtually no background before coming into her classroom, she wasn't able to move her students far enough to correctly answer those questions on the test. With item and strand information, teachers can draw some plausible conclusions about the cumulative effects of the educational program on students in their school, but this information tells them very little about the effectiveness of their grade-level program. To understand the impact of the instruction in their classrooms, they need value-added information.

> Value-added information gives teachers a definitive starting place for improvement.

Value-added analysis sheds light on the progress students make over the course of a single school year. It tells teachers whether the educational program, as it is currently being delivered, is producing the kinds of gains that it should be producing. This information can be surprising, validating, or disappointing for teachers, a subject we delve into more deeply in Chapter 6. A robust value-added analysis also tells teachers whether some of their students grew more than others given the current program. It is this kind of information, in conjunction with the insights from item and strand analysis, that allows teachers to thoughtfully improve both what they are teaching as well as how they are teaching it. For example, a particular teacher may discover through value-added information that his or her students made expected gains in the aggregate but that the growth was uneven across prior achievement subgroups. Low-achieving students grew more than expected while high-achieving students grew less than would be expected. Value-added information gives the teacher a definitive starting place for improvement. In planning for the next school year, the teacher will want to maintain the aspects of the program that work well for her lower achievers but supplement the program to work more effectively with her high achievers.

Concept 3: The District, School, and Classroom Levels Are Interdependent Nested Systems

As we move forward in this chapter it is important to understand that the district, the school, and the classroom are interdependent nested systems. In other words, each of these levels of a school system is made up of interconnected, interdependent parts and the results at one level are, at least in part, implicated in the results at the other levels. In practice, however, these connections between levels are sometimes overlooked or ignored.

> The district, the school, and the classroom are interdependent nested systems.

Teachers close their classroom doors and operate as if they were independent practitioners; principals compete with other principals to make sure that the best and the brightest educators are in their building; superintendents and school boards produce and enact policies that assume that one size fits all. The discontinuities that result from one level of the system essentially ignoring the others make systemic improvement a daunting task. Fortunately, there is a relatively straightforward strategy to keep actions at each of these systemic levels aligned—*educators at each level of a system must analyze and act upon the data that are relevant to their level within the system!* The question is, Why does this produce alignment?

The most important reason that a focus on each level produces alignment is that district-level data are in fact an aggregate of building-level and teacher-level data. When teachers examine and respond to the patterns in their data, the results they generate are reflected not only in their data but also in their building's and district's data. Similarly, when a district-level team analyzes and appropriately acts upon large-scale patterns in the district data, results are implicated at both the building and classroom levels.

Because of the nested character of these systems—each level sitting within or incorporating the other levels—there is no need to approach improvement hierarchically; that is, there is no need to do a district-level analysis before a school does its building-level analysis or before a teacher team does its classroom-level analysis. There is no need for everyone to have the same goals. If each level of the system is appropriately responding to the data at their level, performance of the entire system will improve. Because these systems are nested within one another, an appropriate response at one level will be positively reflected in the data at all the other levels. Given this understanding the remaining question is, How should educators at the district, the school, and the teacher levels analyze and appropriately respond to their data? What actions can educators take at each of these levels that will ultimately result in systemic improvement?

> What actions can educators take at each of these levels that will ultimately result in systemic improvement?

The ABCs of Systemic Improvement

Two of the best known adages about systems are: (1) every system is perfectly designed to get the results it gets, and (2) if we keep doing what we've always done, then we'll continue to get the results we've always gotten. These are not just trite sayings; they are fundamental truths about how the system operates. The upshot of both these adages is simple—the only way to produce different results is to think and act differently. As educators we have to quit blaming the kids, their parents, or the community and begin to change what we think and do, both individually and collectively.

So if systemic improvement is about improving how we think and act, what is it that we should think about and do differently? Any kind of systemic improvement, whether it relates to improving your golf swing, improving the eating habits of your family, or improving the overall achievement level of a school system involves a three-stage process driven by three essential questions: (a) What is the current performance of the system? (b) What are the *root causes* of these results? (c) What do we think about and do differently to improve? These three questions are explored in this chapter and the five chapters that follow.

Concept 4: Objective Information Is Key to Understanding the Current State of the System

What Is the Current Performance of the System?

Regardless of the size or the complexity of a system, it is critical that this first question be addressed with some kind of relatively objective data. Subjective information is essential for making sense of day-to-day events but not for answering this basic systems question. Let's talk about why this is the case.

The systems adage mentioned earlier—every system is perfectly designed to get the results it gets—is at the heart of this issue. A system produces its particular results because of the ways in which its parts interact with one another. These interactions actually produce a whole that is greater than the sum of its parts. In other words, systems produce results that cannot be accounted for by any of the individual parts. As individuals, when we act as a part of a system, we act with partial understanding. To improve a system we must be able to look at it as a whole, that is, from the outside in.

For example, all golfers want to improve their golf games. As they play, they *feel* things going wrong and they try to correct their swings based on these feelings. Typically, however, these efforts produce either no improvement or in many cases poorer results. To create improvement in their swings, they must find ways to get *outside* of the system of which their subjective experience is a part. This is why they need more objective kinds of data, things such as video recordings of their swing taken from different vantage points or an objective assessment by a trained golf coach. The key here is, if you want to improve the performance of a system, you have to find a way of examining that system from the outside in.

> If you want to improve the performance of a system, you have to find a way of examining that system from the outside in.

In the context of this book, then, the relatively objective data that are critical for this first step are the system's achievement and value-added information. As we move toward the second question associated with this process—what are the root causes of these results—there is a significant role for more subjective data, but in this first step it is important to limit attention to the objective data the system generates. It is also important to note that value-added information provides a completely new perspective on the work that educators do. Achievement data provide information on where students are relative to their system's standards. Value-added information, on the other hand, is about the efficacy of the programs that are designed to move students through the standards-based system. In other words, value-added information tells educators how well the current program is working in general and with particular subgroups of students. With value-added information, educators now have what business people have long taken for granted: a relatively trustworthy measure of productivity. Value-added information tells us how productive the current educational program is.

As we think about the achievement and value-added information that are available to educators, it is important to think in terms of both aggregate- and disaggregate-level data. Both kinds of data are important, but each answers different questions with respect to system performance. In Chapters 4, 5, and 6, we will illustrate what these data look like at different levels of a school system and what practitioners at each level should do with both their aggregate- and disaggregate-level data.

Concept 5: Focus on the System—Connecting Levels of Analysis and Stages of Inquiry

If we assemble the pieces we have introduced in this chapter, the result is a three-level, three-stage model for educational improvement. Figure 3.1 is a representation of this model. The three levels of analysis are represented by the three funnels nested one within the other. The largest funnel represents the district level of analysis, the middle-sized funnel represents the school level of analysis, and the smallest funnel represents the classroom level of analysis. The three stages of inquiry displayed in each funnel represent the three essential questions of systemic improvement: (1) What is the current performance of the system? (2) What are the root causes of these results? (3) What do we think and do differently to improve?

Figure 3.1 Focus on the System Process

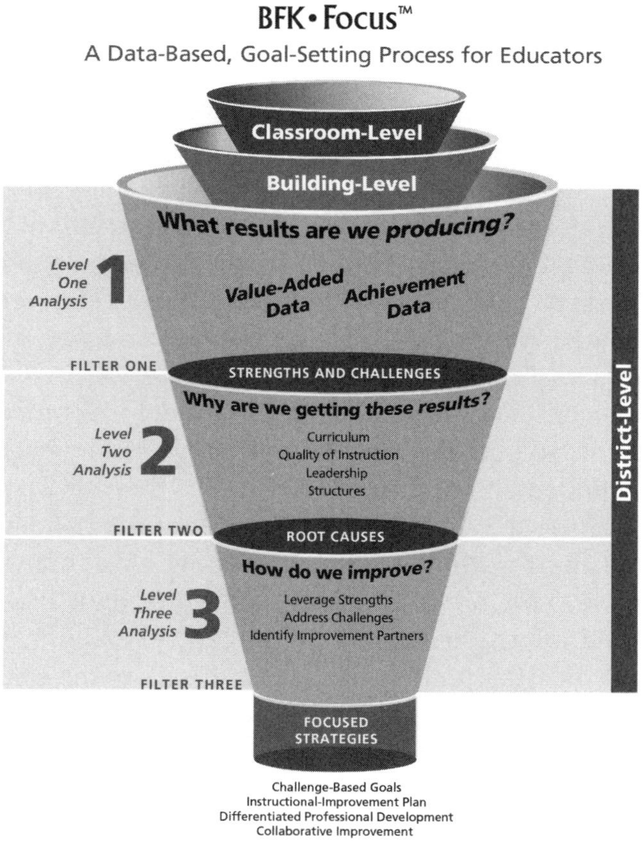
BFK • Focus™
A Data-Based, Goal-Setting Process for Educators
Classroom-Level
Building-Level
What results are we producing?
Level One Analysis 1
Value-Added Data
Achievement Data
FILTER ONE
STRENGTHS AND CHALLENGES
Why are we getting these results?
Level Two Analysis 2
Curriculum
Quality of Instruction
Leadership
Structures
FILTER TWO
ROOT CAUSES
How do we improve?
Level Three Analysis 3
Leverage Strengths
Address Challenges
Identify Improvement Partners
FILTER THREE
FOCUSED STRATEGIES
Challenge-Based Goals
Instructional-Improvement Plan
Differentiated Professional Development
Collaborative Improvement
District-Level

Source: © 2011, Battelle for Kids.

Concept 6: The Importance of Focus

Beyond what has already been discussed in this chapter, there are two other big ideas embedded in the design of this model. The first big idea is conveyed in the name of the process—*focus.* This title emerged both from the literature on educational change and our direct work with clients. The core issue for an improvement team, regardless of whether it operates at the district, the school, or the classroom level, is that there are too many issues to address, too many problems to solve, and too many practices that require improvement. Unfortunately, the result of trying to improve everything is that nothing much improves. Because of this reality, our advice to the members of an improvement team has always been to tackle one, or at most, two big issues in a school year. Any more than that and the likelihood is that not much will get done.

A second reason for insisting on this kind of focus is a consequence of what is known about systems. In many cases, because almost all issues are systems issues, by improving performance in one area, other related things also change, and in most cases, improve. As the systems folks are apt to say, "you can't do one thing." Because everything is connected to everything else, one change almost always produces other kinds of change. There is also a corollary to this consequence of focused change. Any team engaged in improvement must always guard against throwing the baby out with the bath water. In an effort to make things better for one group of students it is imperative that the team not make things worse for another group. So an important question for any team of educators engaged in improvement is, What do we hold onto that works and what do we change that doesn't?

The other big idea embedded in the model is its funnel shape. Whenever we have talked about this model we have always tried to convey movement. Information goes in the top of the funnel where it is processed, filtered, and sifted into the next stage of the analysis. As the resulting information moves through stage two, root causes are explored. This information is then used in stage three to produce the team's improvement agenda. What finally emerges out the other end of each funnel is a course of action that the team members have produced to address a specific and significant area of challenge.

What we are trying to emphasize in the diagram is that educators at each level of the system ask the same set of three questions of the data that pertain directly to them. We are also trying to communicate that each set of inquiries can take place relatively independent of the others. In other words, a teacher team does not have to wait for the district- and building-level teams to meet and make decisions before the teacher team can meet and make decisions.

> Teachers often find that their core issues align nicely with either a school-based or district-based issue because school data and district data are necessarily related to classroom-level data.

But because of the nested nature of this model, teachers often find that their core issues align nicely with either a school-based or district-based issue because school data and district data are necessarily related to classroom-level data. When this kind of alignment occurs, it's a real plus for a teacher team because alignment typically results in more resources directed toward addressing the issue the teacher team has defined.

Summary

There have been many attempts to produce systemic educational improvement, but because of how educational institutions are organized and enacted, reform has been slow and uneven. In recent years, as a result of value-added analysis, a new but critical reform issue has emerged—teacher quality. The thrust of this chapter has been to assemble a systemic reform model that focuses attention on the teacher level but also outlines the kinds of actions that can be taken at other levels of the system to produce lasting improvement. In the next five chapters this reform model will be developed and particularized to each of the levels of a school system.

Action Steps and Reflection Questions

Action Step: Discuss the three core questions of systemic improvement. How are they alike or dissimilar to other school improvement questions you've explored in the past?

1. What is the current performance of the system?
2. What are the root causes of these results?
3. What do we think about and do differently to improve? How can we leverage our core strengths to address our core challenges?

Action Step: Look at the Focus on the System funnel and discuss your team's readiness to go through the school improvement process together.

1. Have you tried a systemic approach to school improvement like this before? What worked? What didn't?
2. The funnel portrays three levels of interdependent nested subsystems. Where will you start? At the district, building, or school level?
3. Will educators in your district be working through all levels of the focus funnel? How will that work?

4

Step II

Assess District-Level Value-Added Reports to Determine Strengths and Challenges

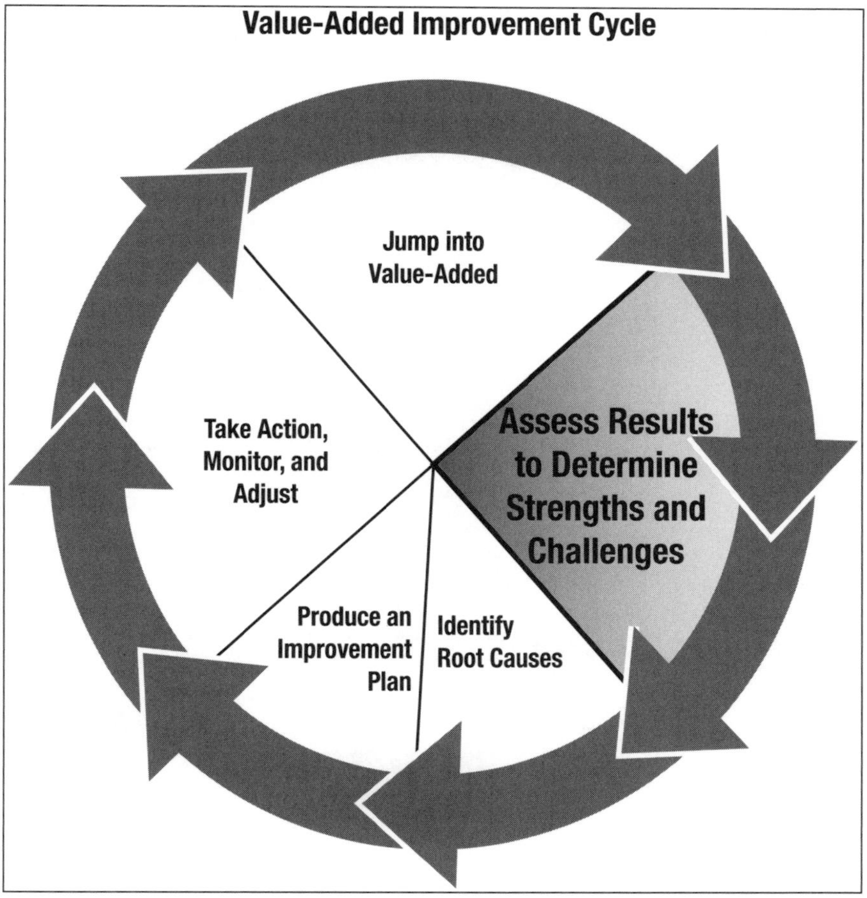

Value-Added Improvement Cycle
Jump into Value-Added
Assess Results to Determine Strengths and Challenges
Identify Root Causes
Produce an Improvement Plan
Take Action, Monitor, and Adjust

Source: © 2011, Battelle for Kids.

Chapter 4 Core Concepts

1. Understand how to read key district-level value-added reports.
2. Produce a Focus on My District matrix to assess current results.
3. Examine disaggregated data to determine strengths and challenges.

Chapter 4 is about digging into district-level data. The BFK•Focus funnel in Figure 4.1 depicts data analysis and improvement processes at the district, school, and classroom levels. You were introduced to the Focus on the System concept in Chapter 3.

At this stage, you will be working with district-level value-added reports along with district-level achievement results to uncover

Figure 4.1 Focus on the System Process

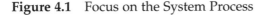

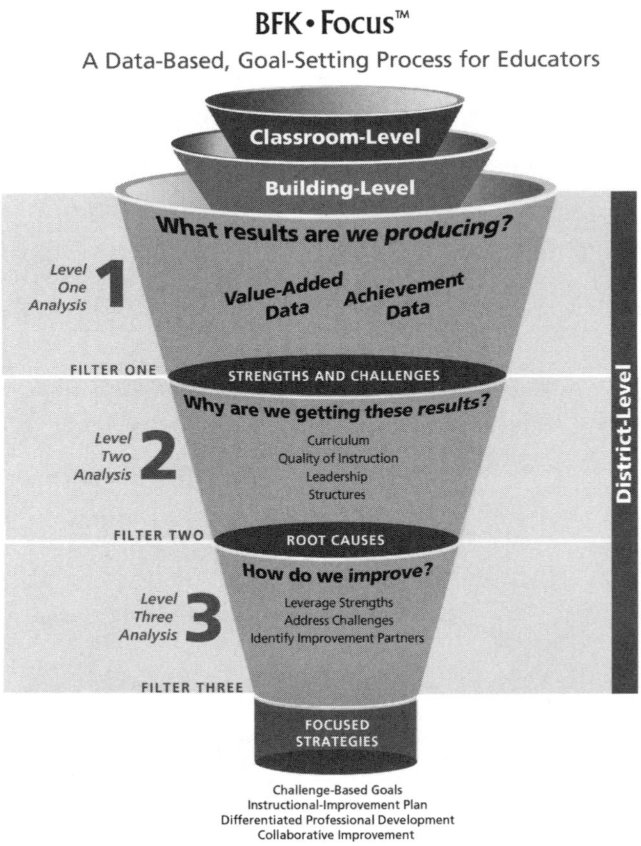
BFK• Focus™
A Data-Based, Goal-Setting Process for Educators
Classroom-Level
Building-Level
What results are we producing?
Level One Analysis 1
Value-Added Data
Achievement Data
FILTER ONE
STRENGTHS AND CHALLENGES
Why are we getting these results?
Level Two Analysis 2
Curriculum
Quality of Instruction
Leadership
Structures
FILTER TWO
ROOT CAUSES
How do we improve?
Level Three Analysis 3
Leverage Strengths
Address Challenges
Identify Improvement Partners
FILTER THREE
FOCUSED STRATEGIES
Challenge-Based Goals
Instructional-Improvement Plan
Differentiated Professional Development
Collaborative Improvement
District-Level

Source: © 2011, Battelle for Kids.

patterns that exist across schools and grades. But before you can work through the stages of the district-level funnel, you must be able to interpret district-level value-added reports. We recommend you look at these reports in a collaborative group, made up of key educators from your district. If possible, include leaders and educators from the various buildings in your district; it's a rare event to bring educators together from across a district to analyze data, but this experience is usually powerful.

Concept 1: Understand How to Read Key District-Level Value-Added Reports

The starting place for this inquiry is your district-level value-added report. Value-added reports are typically provided by outside companies or organizations that specialize in value-added modeling (VAM) and have been contracted by the school district or state education agency to provide educators with annual value-added reports. Some large school districts have enough technical expertise on staff to produce their own value-added models. As a result, the look and form of districts' value-added reports vary.

The report displayed in Figure 4.2 is produced by SAS and is available to districts through the Education Value-Added Assessment System (EVAAS) services of SAS Institute, Inc.

Normal Curve Equivalents: How Are They Different?

Normal curve equivalents (NCEs) are represented on a scale from 1 to 99. This scale coincides with a percentile rank scale at 1, 50, and 99. Unlike percentile rank scores, the interval between scores is equal. This means you can average NCEs to compare groups of students or schools.

To make sense of this district-level value-added report, let's explore some of its key features. This SAS-generated report depicts the district-level value-added results for mathematics across three years from 2008 to 2010 to provide both historical and current information about the value-added gains made in this district relative to the state growth expectation. Value-added growth here is defined as the mean NCE gain and expressed using NCE scores. An NCE scale is similar to a percentile scale, but unlike a percentile scale, an

Figure 4.2 District Value-Added Report (Math)

2010 District Value-Added Report
ABC District
Math

Estimated District Mean NCE Gain							
Grade	3	4	5	6	7	8	Mean NCE Gain over Grades Relative to Growth Standard
Growth Standard		0.0	0.0	0.0	0.0	0.0	
2008 Mean NCE Gain		2.7 G*	-2.1 R	1.8 G*	5.4 G*	-5.2 R*	0.6
Std Error		1.3	1.2	1.1	1.1	1.0	0.5
2009 Mean NCE Gain		6.0 G*	-1.5 R	1.8 G*	4.0 G*	-3.2 R*	1.5
Std Error		1.1	1.2	1.2	1.1	1.1	0.5
2010 Mean NCE Gain		-2.1 R*	-5.2 R*	-4.7 R*	-5.4 R*	-13.4 R*	-6.1
Std Error		1.2	1.1	1.2	1.2	1.0	0.5
3-Yr-Avg. NCE Gain		2.2 G*	-2.7 R*	-0.3 Y	1.4 G*	-7.2 R*	-1.3
Std Error		0.7	0.7	0.7	0.7	0.6	0.2
Estimated District Mean NCE Scores							
Grade	3	4	5	6	7	8	
District Base Year (2007)	50.0	50.0	50.0	50.0	50.0	50.0	
2007 Mean	57.7	56.8	48.9	51.8	58.3	55.1	
2008 Mean	51.4	60.3	54.7	50.7	57.2	53.1	
2009 Mean	56.9	57.4	58.8	56.5	54.6	54.0	
2010 Mean	51.3	54.8	52.2	54.1	51.1	41.2	

	G* - Estimated mean NCE gain is above the growth standard by at least 1 standard error.
	G* - Estimated mean NCE gain is equal to or greater than growth standard but by less than 1 standard error.
	Y - Estimated mean NCE gain is below the growth standard by 1 standard error or less.
	R - Estimated mean NCE gain is more than 1 standard error below the growth standard but by 2 standard errors or less.
	R* - Estimated mean NCE gain is below the growth standard by more than 2 standard errors.

Source: SAS® EVAAS® for K–12 content Copyright ©2011, SAS Institute Inc., Cary, NC, USA, All Rights Reserved. Used with permission.

NCE scale is an equal interval scale. This equal interval property makes this scale useful for comparisons across multiple years of analysis and across multiple subject areas. For example, with NCE scores, a three-year average gain can be calculated.

This view of a district's value-added results helps to answer one essential question: How much growth was produced grade level by grade level across the district? With some additional step-by-step exploration, we can make better sense of this data display and determine the answer.

Steps to Reading Your Value-Added Reports

Step 1: Understand the estimated mean NCE scores.
Step 2: Determine yearly mean gains.
Step 3: Determine 3-year-average mean gains.
Step 4: Determine the magnitude of the gain relative to the growth standard.

Step 1: Understand the Estimated Mean NCE Scores

If you look at the district's estimated mean scores for 2010, you see that the average seventh-grade student scored at 51.1 NCEs relative to the state. This places the average seventh grader in the district slightly above the average achievement level for the state relative to the state's standard setting year of 2007. The performance of this same student cohort can be tracked backward through time by going up the diagonal to the left. The average student in this cohort scored 56.5 NCEs as a sixth grader in 2009, 54.7 NCEs as a fifth grader in 2008, and 56.8 NCEs as a fourth grader in 2006. So, over this four-year period, this cohort of students has not maintained its relative achievement level.

Step 2: Determine Yearly Mean Gains

When you look at the 2010 mean NCE gain for seventh grade, you see the number –5.4 and the letter R*. The number –5.4 denotes the change from a mean score of 56.5 NCEs (estimated mean for sixth graders in 2009) to a mean of 51.1 as seventh graders in 2010. The R* symbol (and the red color of the cell in a full color table) stands for *red*, which indicates that the mean gain is at least two standard errors below expected. Although the images here are black and white, oftentimes a color-coded system is used to denote below-expected gains, above-expected gains, or gains that are within the expected range. The determination of what constitutes these levels is a policy decision; therefore, these designations vary from state to state and district to district.

What Is Standard Error?

Standard error is a measure of the uncertainty associated with an estimation of a mean student gain. Generally speaking, the smaller the standard error, the more precise the estimate of gain. The size or magnitude of the standard error is influenced by both the size of the student cohort and the standard deviation of scores around the mean. Typically, the larger the student cohort, the smaller the standard error, and the larger the range of scores, the larger the standard error.

Step 3: Determine Three-Year-Average Mean Gains

In the row labeled 3-Yr-Avg. NCE Gain in Figure 4.2, SAS EVAAS offers information about the average gain made over the last three years in each grade level. Here you see that the seventh graders averaged 1.4 NCEs of gain across each of the last three years. It is helpful to look at the three-year average to get a more reliable picture of program effectiveness over time.

Step 4: Determine the Magnitude of the Gain Relative to the Growth Standard

In 2010, the mean NCE gain across Grades 4 through 8 was –6.1 with a standard error of 0.5. This means that there is a high level of certainty that the average student across grade levels made significantly less progress than expected in 2010.

Answering the Essential Question

Your interpretation of these data should reveal the answer to an essential question: How much growth was produced grade level by grade level across your district? From this information you can see that on average, the district made considerably less than expected growth in mathematics in 2010. This observation is important for a district leadership team to consider. They can further explore why there is a downward trend and consistently poor results in the eighth grade as they proceed through the BFK•Focus process.

Pause to Practice

Use the value-added report for math above to answer these questions:

1. Which grade level has the highest estimated mean achievement level for 2010? The lowest?
2. Which grade level produced the most growth in math in 2010? The least?
3. In terms of student gains in math, how well did the district perform as a whole in 2009?

Answers appear at the end of this chapter.

Concept 2: Produce a Focus on My District Matrix to Assess Current Results

Once the value-added results have been analyzed, the district team should examine the relationship between progress and achievement. When a district-level leadership team is assembled to analyze its data, team members must keep in mind that their ultimate objective is not just to understand but also to act. Remember, if you keep doing what you've always done, then you'll continue to get the results you've always gotten. This means taking thoughtful and appropriate action, not simply telling others to solve the problem. But in taking action, the district team must consciously act at the level of the system where it can reasonably influence results. For example, a district team has little capacity to go into every classroom to coach teachers toward more effective practice, but if their data reveal that the district as a whole is struggling to produce growth with high achieving students, a district team can arrange for district-wide professional development that helps all teachers become more effective with high achieving students. The underlying premise here is that a district team has more capacity to impact large-scale patterns than the more idiosyncratic patterns that appear at the building or classroom levels. In terms of its aggregate-level data, a district-level team should ask specific questions:

- In which areas are current student performance results the strongest? Which areas are the strongest over time?

- In which areas are current results the weakest? Which areas are weakest over time?
- In which areas are results stagnant?

These are all critical questions because they focus attention on large-scale systemic patterns. They indicate where educators have been especially effective and where improvement is necessary. One of the best and simplest tools for answering these kinds of questions is what we call the Focus on My District matrix. With this tool, value-added gains are plotted on one axis, and mean achievement levels are plotted on the other axis. The beauty of this simple tool is that it allows a district team to view two different educational dimensions (progress and achievement) simultaneously. A sample Focus on My District matrix is displayed in Figure 4.3.

Figure 4.3 Focus on My District Matrix

Achievement (Mean NCE Score)	Q1	Q2	Q3	Q4	Q5
> 58					4th Social St. 7th Social St.
52-58	5th Math 6th Math 5th Reading 6th Reading	4th Math 5th Social St	4th Reading 6th Social St	7th Reading	4th Science
48-52	7th Math 8th Reading 5th Science 8th Social St			7th Science	
42-48	6th Science 8th Science				
< 42	8th Math				
2009-2010	Q1	Q2	Q3	Q4	Q5
	Value-Added (Mean NCE Gain)				

In the Focus on My District matrix, value-added gains are represented along the horizontal, or *x*-axis, or at the bottom of the grid. Growth percentile scores, mean gain scores, or color-coded schemes (such as green for above expected gains, red for below expected gains, and yellow for expected gains) can be used to represent the value-added gain score bands. In this particular version of the Focus on my District matrix, value-added gains are represented by color-coded gain bands. The mean achievement level for each grade level and subject area is located along the vertical, or *y*-axis, and is represented here in terms of NCE bands, with 50 being the mean achievement level in the standard setting year. An NCE score above 50 indicates an above-average mean achievement level; an NCE score below 50 indicates a below-average mean achievement level. The greater the departure from 50 NCEs, the more significantly high or low is the average achievement level. The bands on the achievement axis could also be represented in different ways, for example, by achievement test percentiles, test score ranges, or other calculated measures of performance (such as a weighted achievement measure).

This simple rendering of two different kinds of data provides a wealth of information. The greatest aggregate-level strengths for this particular district are represented in the top right-hand corner of the matrix. These are the grade level and subject areas that reflect both high levels of achievement and high levels of growth. For this district, fourth-grade science and social studies and seventh-grade reading and social studies are clear areas of strength. Instead of simply taking note of these results, district leaders should focus attention on why these particular program areas are so effective. How are the curricular and instructional patterns in these areas producing above-expected results?

Areas in the bottom left-hand quadrant of the matrix require a different kind of attention. The grade levels and subject areas in this part of the matrix indicate both low achievement and low value-added gains. Why? Why are the sixth-grade science and eighth-grade math and science programs not working for students? What is it about the current educational program that is producing below-expected results?

There are two other areas of this matrix that tell a particular story. The grade level and subject areas in the top-left part of the matrix represent program areas in which students' average achievement level may be high, but growth is in fact below expectations. These are very likely grade level and subject areas in which practice has become overly routinized or stagnant. The educators in these areas likely believe they are effective because their students are passing the test, but the truth of the matter is that most of their success can be traced back to prior teachers and/or a home life that is providing high-quality educational resources. The educators in these program areas are in need of some stretch goals associated with the growth of their students.

The last piece of the matrix, the lower right-hand corner, represents those program areas in which students are experiencing more than expected growth but are, on average, still below expected achievement levels. Notice that our sample district has no program areas in this part of the matrix. Typically, large urban districts will have some of their curricular areas fall into this part of the matrix. Instead of sanctioning the programs in this part of the matrix, we should study them. Educators in these program areas have figured out how to produce substantial growth with students who enter school in the fall well behind their age-group peers.

It is also possible to see other patterns that go beyond a quadrant-based analysis. By color-coding entries by subject area, the district team can easily see subject area patterns. In the district, mathematics is a real area of concern. All five of the district's Grades 4 through 8 math courses are in the first two columns. In other words, none of the Grades 4 through 8 math courses are producing even expected levels of growth. So, in terms of large-scale patterns, mathematics is a real concern.

The same data could also be color-coded by grade level, revealing relatively strong programs in fourth and seventh grades and relatively ineffective programs at the other grade levels.

Concept 3: Examine Disaggregated Data to Determine Strengths and Challenges

The district team should also examine its disaggregated data, or data broken down into subgroups, to look for other kinds of patterns. There are many cases, for example, when a good curriculum does not work well for all students and an ineffective curriculum works well for some students. The only way to know this for sure is to examine disaggregated growth information that displays growth patterns for different student subgroups. In Figure 4.5 you see the graphic component of a set of district diagnostic reports associated with our sample district's problematic math results. There are numerical data that accompany these graphic reports, but the graphic results are sufficient to see important patterns.

The reports displayed in Figure 4.4 are produced by SAS and are available to districts through the EVAAS services of SAS Institute, Inc.

Figure 4.4 District Diagnostic Reports (Math)

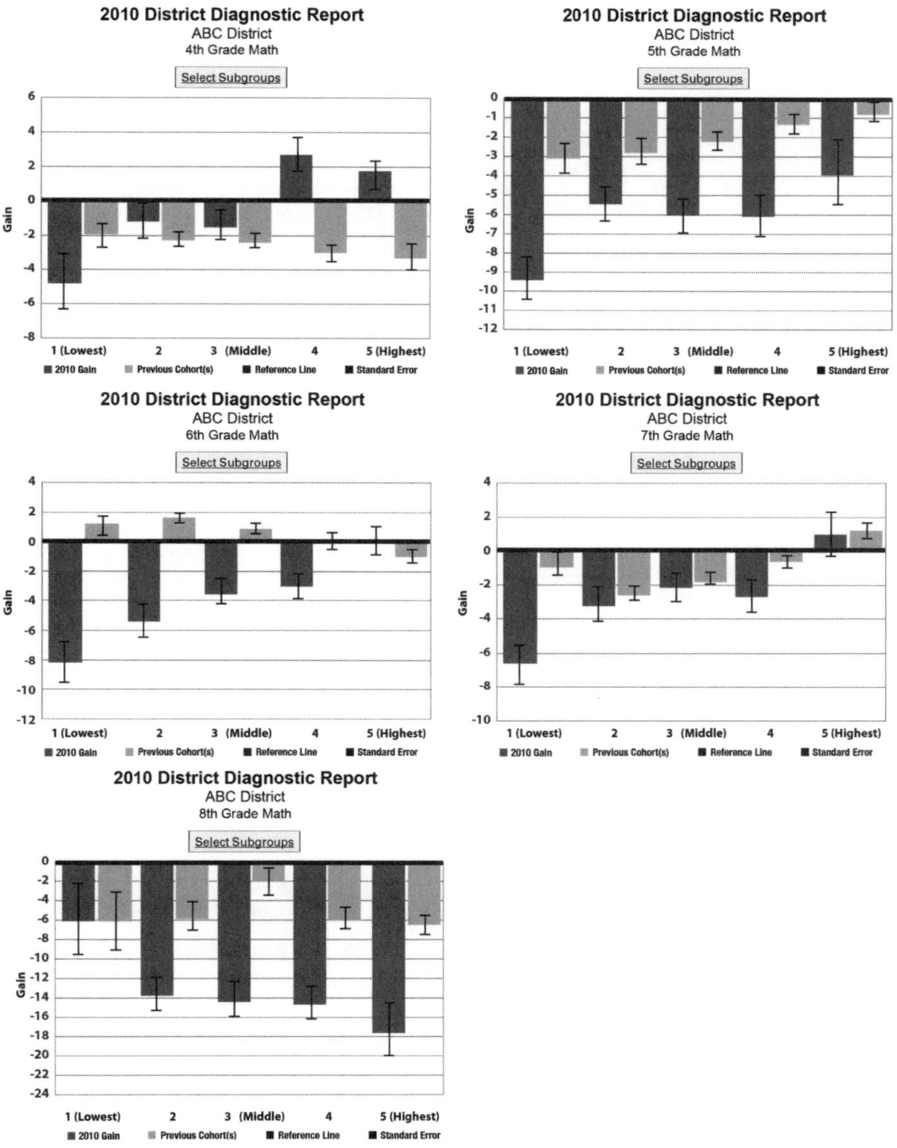
2010 District Diagnostic Report
ABC District
4th Grade Math
Select Subgroups
Gain
1 (Lowest)
2
3 (Middle)
4
5 (Highest)
2010 Gain
Previous Cohort(s)
Reference Line
Standard Error
2010 District Diagnostic Report
ABC District
5th Grade Math
Select Subgroups
Gain
1 (Lowest)
2
3 (Middle)
4
5 (Highest)
2010 Gain
Previous Cohort(s)
Reference Line
Standard Error
2010 District Diagnostic Report
ABC District
6th Grade Math
Select Subgroups
Gain
1 (Lowest)
2
3 (Middle)
4
5 (Highest)
2010 Gain
Previous Cohort(s)
Reference Line
Standard Error
2010 District Diagnostic Report
ABC District
7th Grade Math
Select Subgroups
Gain
1 (Lowest)
2
3 (Middle)
4
5 (Highest)
2010 Gain
Previous Cohort(s)
Reference Line
Standard Error
2010 District Diagnostic Report
ABC District
8th Grade Math
Select Subgroups
Gain
1 (Lowest)
2
3 (Middle)
4
5 (Highest)
2010 Gain
Previous Cohort(s)
Reference Line
Standard Error

Source: SAS® EVAAS® for K–12 content Copyright ©2011, SAS Institute Inc., Cary, NC, USA, All Rights Reserved. Used with permission.

The darkest grey-toned bars in the five graphic representations shown in Figure 4.5 represent the most recent subgroups of students in our sample school district. In each report, the dark bar on the far left represents the students in the district whose achievement level would be in the bottom 20% of the state. Similarly, the dark bar on the far right of each graph represents the students in the district whose achievement level would place them in the top 20% of the state.

Figure 4.5 District Diagnostic Reports (Fourth Grade)

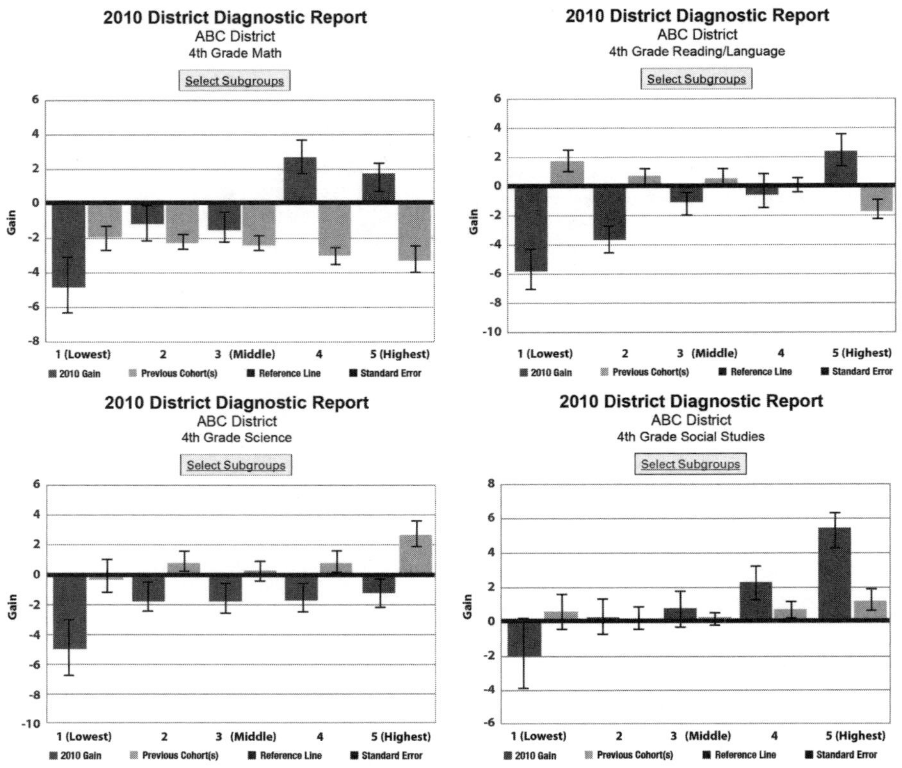
2010 District Diagnostic Report
ABC District
4th Grade Math
Select Subgroups
Gain
1 (Lowest)
2
3 (Middle)
4
5 (Highest)
2010 Gain
Previous Cohort(s)
Reference Line
Standard Error
2010 District Diagnostic Report
ABC District
4th Grade Reading/Language
Select Subgroups
Gain
1 (Lowest)
2
3 (Middle)
4
5 (Highest)
2010 Gain
Previous Cohort(s)
Reference Line
Standard Error
2010 District Diagnostic Report
ABC District
4th Grade Science
Select Subgroups
Gain
1 (Lowest)
2
3 (Middle)
4
5 (Highest)
2010 Gain
Previous Cohort(s)
Reference Line
Standard Error
2010 District Diagnostic Report
ABC District
4th Grade Social Studies
Select Subgroups
Gain
1 (Lowest)
2
3 (Middle)
4
5 (Highest)
2010 Gain
Previous Cohort(s)
Reference Line
Standard Error

The other three bars represent students in the other three quintile-based subgroups. The lighter grey-colored bars in each graph represent the same information for prior cohorts of students. The thick horizontal line in each graph represents the expected progress level for each student subgroup. The dark and light bars that stretch below this line represent student subgroups that experienced less than expected progress, whereas dark and light bars above this line represent student subgroups that experienced more than expected progress. In all cases, the further above or below the thick line, the more pronounced the growth above or below the expected level.

As the district team examines its math results across grade levels (Figure 4.4), the team is looking for any kind of consistent pattern in the data. Are there large-scale subgroup strengths that can be leveraged at the district level? Are there large-scale challenges that are better addressed at the district level? In the data analysis process described in this chapter, this kind of pattern finding is essential. Where there are consistent large-scale patterns, large-scale action can and should be taken. Where there are no clear patterns at the district level, strengths and challenges should be addressed at the level in which they arise.

In the case of these data we see a relatively consistent pattern: With the exception of the eighth-grade data, lower achieving students are experiencing less growth, relatively speaking, than their higher achieving peers. And, in eighth grade, where the opposite pattern is seen, low achieving students are also experiencing less than expected growth. So, in terms of strengths, this district is doing a relatively good job of producing growth with its high achieving math students. Eighth grade is the obvious exception to this pattern. Similarly, in terms of challenges, this district's math program is doing a poor job of producing growth with its lowest achieving students. These students are losing ground to their low-achieving peers across the state.

Once the math analysis is complete the district team would do a similar vertical analysis of the disaggregated information associated with reading, science, and social studies (see Figure 4.5).

Once the district team has examined its data vertically—looking for patterns in its disaggregated data in each subject area from Grades 4 through 8—it examines the same data horizontally, that is, within grade levels. In Figure 4.5, you see the set of four diagnostic reports associated with each tested subject area in the fourth grade.

The reports displayed in Figure 4.5 are produced by SAS and are available to districts through the EVAAS services of SAS Institute, Inc.

The purpose of this analysis is to look for patterns within grade levels. Clearly visible in this set of fourth-grade diagnostic reports is the same kind of pattern that characterized the math reports across grade levels. In general, lower achieving students are making less progress than higher achieving students. When the analysis of fourth-grade reports is completed, the district team goes through the same process for the disaggregated data associated with each of the other grade levels.

Establishing District Priorities

It is not enough for a district-level team to know what its current strengths and challenges are. The next question is, how will the team leverage its strengths to address its challenges? A team's ability to successfully leverage its strengths or overcome its challenges is predicated on its capacity to prioritize and focus its work. The more a team tries to spread its attention across multiple strengths and/or multiple challenges, the less likely the team is to create real substantive change. Change takes work, and work requires focus. We recommend that a team take on no more than two large-scale challenges in any given year. One is best, but two may be manageable. The whole purpose of looking for patterns in the data is to find an area where concerted effort can yield measurable results. The key to productive change is to focus efforts on a goal worth pursuing.

When the district team has examined and found patterns in both its aggregate information (Focus on the System matrix) and its disaggregated information (vertically and horizontally organized disaggregated data reports), the team should rank order its district-level strengths and prioritize its district-level challenges with the thought of choosing a minimal number of high-leverage goals to pursue. Ultimately, the team identifies one or two strengths and one or two challenges that are noteworthy in terms of their expansiveness and/or magnitude. In the next level of analysis, in which the team explores the *root causes* of its current state, strengths are important because the practices that produce them may also be used to address areas of challenge.

We end this chapter with the story of a transformed teaching and learning organization. Susie Bailey, the curriculum director in the rural Ohio community of Washington Court House tells of her district's efforts to overcome low performance and low growth. Their journey exemplifies how district leaders can put value-added information to work and how, as a result, they have demonstrated high levels of student progress. This story continues to inspire our work and hopefully will inspire readers to further explore using progress and achievement data to establish improvement priorities. In the next chapter we examine these data at the building level.

One District's Success Story: Washington Court House City Schools, Ohio

Susie Bailey, Director, Curriculum, Assessment, and Data

District: 2,389 students, 4 schools, approximately 50% poverty, approximately 20% Individualized Education Program (IEP) students

Living and working for the past three years in Washington Court House City Schools has felt like riding a bullet train. We recently discovered the astonishing news that we are in the top 10% of public districts in Ohio in terms of student progress. Just two years earlier, 2008 progress data placed us in the bottom 5% of public districts. We are just about to take Dr. Mary Peters's advice and have a parade!

At last summer's leadership retreat, we reflected on the BFK•Focus funnel and realized that through our lightning-paced school improvement journey, we have addressed every issue suggested in the improvement process and more. In this period of time, we have for the first time aligned the entire curriculum to the academic content standards, and 100% of our teachers have received formative assessment and data team training. We have modified all our building schedules to allow more time for reading and math as well as time within the school day for intervention and enrichment. We implemented Professional Learning Communities (PLCs) and carved out time for the PLCs to meet through monthly late starts across the district. Teachers received professional development in powerful, research-based instructional strategies as well as in accurate grading and reporting practices. Administrators and some teachers are regularly performing walk-throughs to monitor expectations and offer feedback. More IEP students are receiving access to the regular curriculum, and the high school and middle school administrators have worked together to create a transition plan to support students who are at risk for dropping out. Our high school is participating in the BFK value-added high school project with its accompanying value-added and formative assessment training, and our primary school teachers are receiving ongoing professional development on how to analyze assessment data to provide effective reading instruction.

My training as a regional value-added specialist (RVAS) was invaluable preparation for my current position as director of curriculum, data, and assessment. Mike Thomas gave me a place to start long before I moved into central office when he came to our district to analyze our district's dismal scores. I recall that it took him only a matter of minutes to examine our achievement and value-added data and to determine the crux of the problem. He looked up at the assembled principals and central office administrators and stated simply, "Your curriculum is not aligned." Years later, when it was my turn, I knew what I had to do first. With the help of my former RVAS colleagues from state support centers and my central office teammates, the mission was accomplished.

Value-added reporting was our first attempt at looking beyond whether 75% of our students at a given grade level and subject area had passed the state tests. Teachers have learned to determine which grade levels and subject areas are making growth. Using value-added subgroup information, they discovered which groups of students were receiving the most benefit from their instruction. Teachers now anticipate and enjoy looking at data about their classes and individual students to compare the students' predicted and observed scores. They understand that projections are a powerful feature of their value-added reporting and look forward to receiving those reports as soon as they become available each fall. These projections are used for student placement decisions, especially into higher level courses, and help us determine which students need intervention. Using the BFK Focus process to guide discussions around the data, teachers share their successes as well as their instructional and assessment strategies.

Our high school has also received tremendous benefit from our relationship with Battelle for Kids (BFK). When BFK received a grant from the Bill and Melinda Gates Foundation to pilot end-of-course exams, our district jumped at the opportunity to participate and get value-added data at the high school for the very first time. After a year of administering the tests and comparing our results with other schools, we were chosen to participate in a *deeper dive* experience that has allowed us to move to another level in our effort to increase student achievement. Through the BFK formative assessment training and on-site support, we have made monitoring of student progress the focus of our building improvement plan. The participating teachers and the rest of our core academic teachers studied online formative assessment modules and are currently applying those principles in their classrooms. The high school's leadership team's focus is now on formative assessments, including accurate grading and reporting. The high school pilot experience has been revolutionary, not only at that level but also across the entire district. Our high school principal, Jeff Hodson, continues to work closely with his key teachers and BFK personnel to create and to communicate about building-wide assessment, grading, and reporting policies. The high school is the undisputed district leader in this area.

The entire climate of our district has changed. Four years ago, we were a textbook case for teacher isolation. As an example, a distressed teacher came to me when I was a counselor and asked for advice about how to deal with a teacher down the hall who was coming into her room after she left at night and stealing her lesson plans. Many teachers were pining for days gone by and living for the day when *THE test* would go away. The prevailing attitude among many staff members was that it was unfair to hold them accountable for results when our kids were as unintelligent as their uncaring parents. Worksheets and full-length movies were, for some, the favored form of instruction. Data were rarely used for decision making. Family names were often all the evidence needed to guide instruction for certain students. Special education was characterized by pull-out programs, especially in reading and math classes where the greatest gaps already existed.

I'm grateful those days are behind us. It staggers me to think how far we have come in three years. It has been painful at times. We have often been criticized for not waiting for teacher buy-in. We believe, however, that when research clearly shows that a strategy is effective it would be malpractice not to act. In the immortal words of Robert Frost, "We have miles to go before we sleep," but our trajectory is headed in the right direction. Our state gain index for 2010 indicated that we are in the 94th percentile of all 610 public school districts. That is up from the 45th percentile in 2009 and up from the bottom five percent of districts in 2007.

Our superintendent, Keith Brown, has led a radical climate change in Washington Court House City Schools, beginning with our belief system. He has insisted that we maintain a guaranteed and viable curriculum. He has been adamant that in looking for solutions, we focus on the adults in the system. Under his leadership, we have turned our attention to people and practices—not programs. The strong, cohesive administrative team that Mr. Brown has created in the central office and with building administrators promotes healthy risk taking and provides support for everyone in the system. If I were forced to identify one factor that has made the biggest difference in our growth, teacher efficacy would be at the top of the list. Each one of our carefully designed school improvement efforts has led to incremental, if not small, degrees of success. The traditional belief that schools have little effect on student achievement has crumbled slightly. Once teachers started to see results and began to accept the preponderance of evidence showing that their actions have the greatest impact on student growth, there has been no stopping them.

Summary

In this chapter, we focused on guiding you through the interpretation of district-level reports and using that information to construct a Focus on the System matrix. This matrix serves to quickly and easily summarize the relationships between achievement and progress, while making evident subjects and grades in which strengths and challenges lie. From this analysis you can detect grade-level and subject-area patterns of performance. This knowledge prompts the next stage of analysis—looking for patterns in disaggregated data to determine which student groups are benefiting most and least from the instructional program that is in place. We cannot overstate the importance of spending time with reports that provide disaggregated information.

Pause to Practice Answers

Use the 2010 Value-Added Report for math above to answer the following questions:

1. Which grade level has the highest mean achievement level for 2010? The lowest?

A: Grade 4 has the highest mean achievement level for 2010, and Grade 7 has the lowest.

2. Which grade level produced the most growth in math in 2010? The least?

A: Grade 4 produced the most growth in math in 2010, and Grade 8 produced the least growth.

3. In terms of student gains in math, how well did the district perform as a whole in 2009?

A: Overall, the gains made by students were similar to those in 2008 and superior to those achieved in 2010.

Action Steps and Reflection Questions

Action Step: Print out all of the district-level reports that you have available, and make copies for your district leadership team.
Action Step: Assemble your district leadership team, and devote at least two hours to analyzing your district-level data.

- Have you included educators from across the district?
- Have you included a leader and a teacher representative from each building?
- Does your district leadership team have the tools and resources it needs to be successful in assessing the current results and determining strengths and challenges? You might want to revisit Chapters 1 through 3 to make sure that you've introduced everyone to value-added analysis and that they understand how it fits in a school improvement context.

Action Step: Produce a Focus on My District matrix.

- In which areas are your student performance results the strongest?
- In which areas are they the weakest?
- In which areas are your results stagnant?
- What grade level or subject area results surprised you?
- Which results confirmed your beliefs?

Action Step: Examine your disaggregated data vertically to look for patterns in your math, reading, science, and social studies results.

- What are the patterns of strength in your math, reading, science, and social studies programs?
- What are the patterns of weakness in your math, reading, science, and social studies programs?

Action Step: Examine your disaggregated data horizontally to look for patterns in your grade level math, reading, science, and social studies results.

- What are the patterns of strength in each grade level?
- What are the patterns of weakness in each grade level?

Hands-On Resource Guide for Teachers and Leaders

- Focus on My District Matrix: Template (see Figure 4.6)

Figure 4.6 Focus on My District Matrix: Template

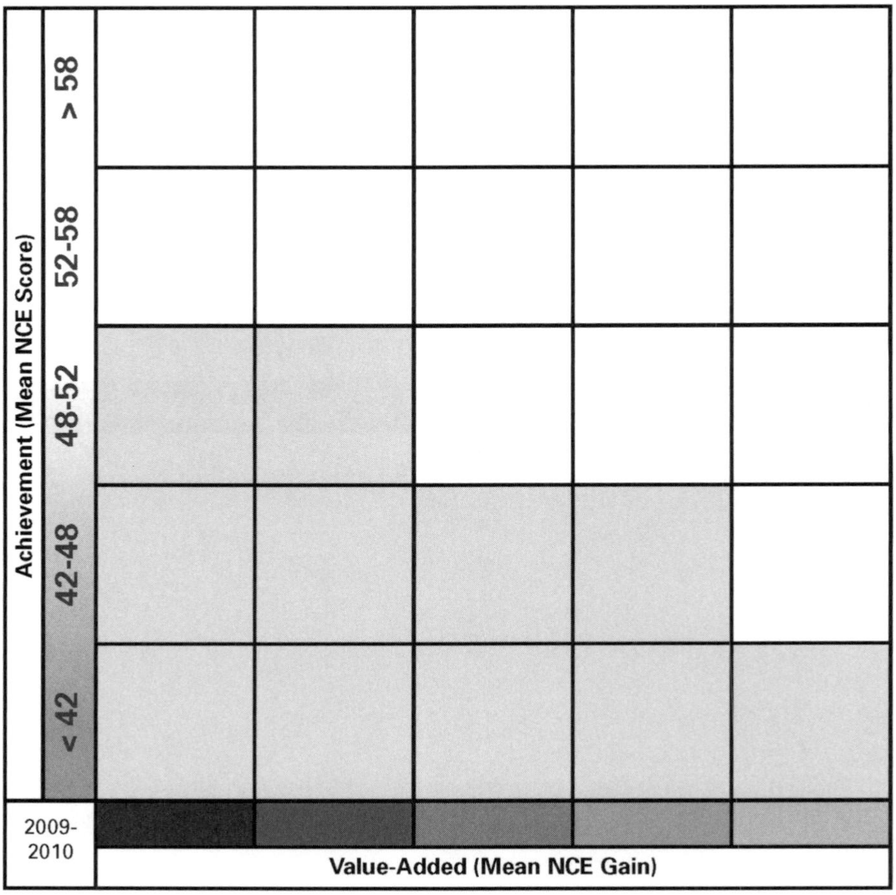
Achievement (Mean NCE Score)
> 58
52-58
48-52
42-48
< 42
2009-2010
Value-Added (Mean NCE Gain)

5

Step II

Assess Building-Level Value-Added Reports to Determine Strengths and Challenges

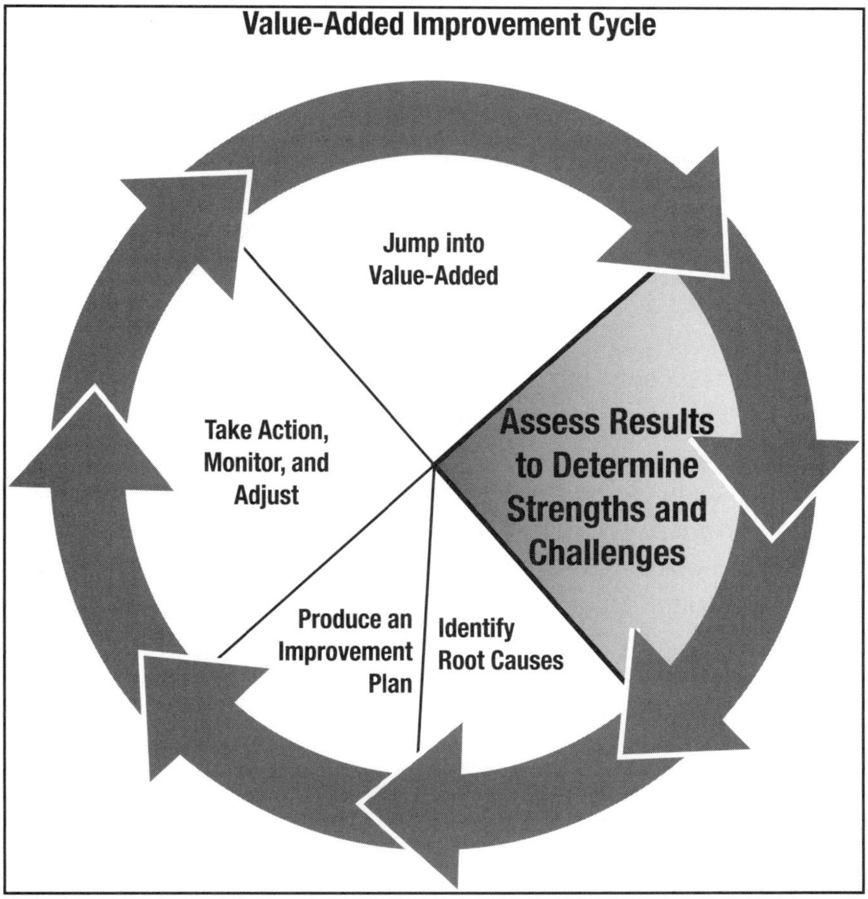
Value-Added Improvement Cycle
Jump into Value-Added
Assess Results to Determine Strengths and Challenges
Identify Root Causes
Produce an Improvement Plan
Take Action, Monitor, and Adjust

Source: © 2011, Battelle for Kids.

Chapter 5 Core Concepts

1. Understand how to read building-level value-added reports.
2. Produce a Focus on My Building matrix to assess current results.
3. Examine disaggregated data to determine strength and challenges.

Before the start of each school year, Bobby Moore, principal of a rural Ohio school district, and his building leadership team planned a data celebration. They lined the walls of the gymnasium with graphs and charts that depict the results the building achieved the previous school year and in years prior. One year, they even used an Academy Awards theme. Sporting a tuxedo, Bobby celebrated the school's strengths by handing out Oscar-like trophies. This beginning-of-the-year celebration was not designed to passively admire the data displays but to carefully examine trends and patterns and to systematically explore the strengths and challenges that emerge.

Bobby shared building achievement and value-added results to reveal whether the strategies he and his staff employed were successful and with whom. In this chapter, we delve into building-level data analysis that begins with interpreting value-added information specific to the school level and move through the stages of the Focus on My Building matrix. We have been describing a single system for uncovering strengths and challenges and isolating improvement priorities through the Focus on the System process. The building-level process closely mirrors the district-level process described in Chapter 4. This chapter addresses the second layer, or building level, of the BFK•Focus funnel depicted in Figure 5.1.

At this stage of the process, you will be working with building-level achievement and value-added reports to uncover patterns that exist across subjects and grades within a school. In this chapter, we bring you through stage one of the building-level BFK•Focus process by addressing how to interpret aggregate- and disaggregate-level value-added and achievement data to identify school-level strengths and challenges.

Concept 1: Understand How to Read Building-Level Value-Added Reports

The first report to become familiar with is your building- or school-level value-added report. Given that value-added reports

Figure 5.1 Focus on the System Process

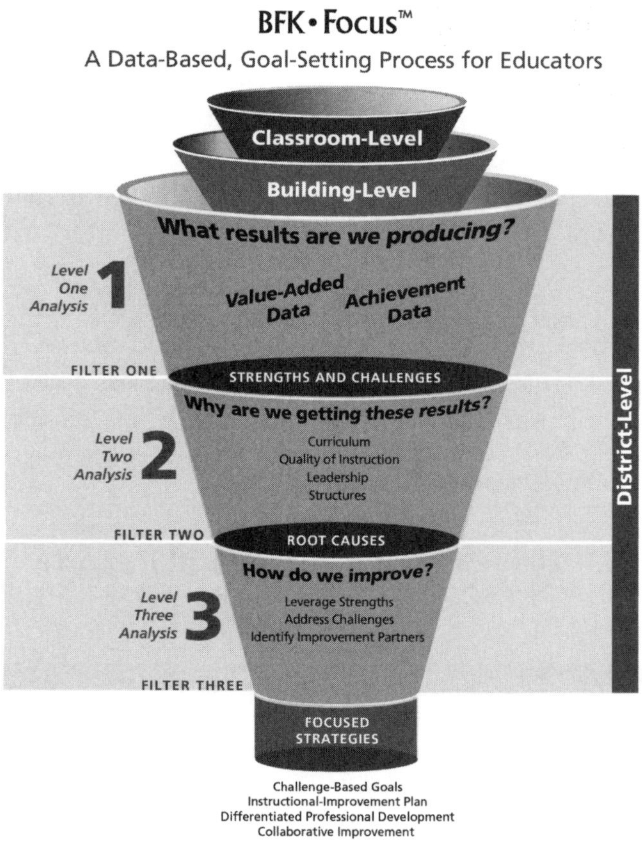
BFK • Focus™
A Data-Based, Goal-Setting Process for Educators
Classroom-Level
Building-Level
What results are we producing?
Level One Analysis 1
Value-Added Data
Achievement Data
FILTER ONE
STRENGTHS AND CHALLENGES
Why are we getting these results?
Level Two Analysis 2
Curriculum
Quality of Instruction
Leadership
Structures
FILTER TWO
ROOT CAUSES
How do we improve?
Level Three Analysis 3
Leverage Strengths
Address Challenges
Identify Improvement Partners
FILTER THREE
FOCUSED STRATEGIES
Challenge-Based Goals
Instructional-Improvement Plan
Differentiated Professional Development
Collaborative Improvement
District-Level

Source: © 2011, Battelle for Kids.

are typically provided by various outside companies or organizations that specialize in value-added modeling (VAM), the look and form of a school's value-added reports may vary. Nonetheless, building-level value-added reports are typically available in mathematics and language arts and oftentimes in science and social studies. Because of federal accountability standards, value-added reports are most frequently generated in Grades 4 through 8, but they can also be generated at the high school level, provided school districts administer common end-of-course assessments. We have found that principals, school literacy coaches, math coaches, and classroom teachers find value-added information very enlightening. More importantly, once they are exposed to a process for interpreting their results and setting priorities, they are galvanized to action.

School Value-Added Reports

This first school value-added report shown in Figure 5.2 is produced by SAS and is available to districts through Education Value-Added Assessment System (EVASS) services of SAS Institute, Inc. This report should be familiar to you as it is almost identical to the district-level report depicted in Chapter 4.

This report depicts building-level results for mathematics in ABC Middle School from 2008 to 2010. To make better sense of this school's data, we first recommend that you turn back to Chapter 4 to refamiliarize yourself with key terms and report features. Recall that the top portion of the table (labeled Estimated School Mean NCE Gain) provides information about student progress across grade levels and school years, and the bottom portion of the table (labeled

Figure 5.2 School Value-Added Report (Math)

2010 School Value-Added Report
ABC Middle School in ABC District
Math

Estimated School Mean NCE Gain					
Grade	5	6	7	8	Mean NCE Gain over Grades Relative to Growth Standard
Growth Standard	0.0	0.0	0.0	0.0	
2008 Mean NCE Gain	-3.2 R*	5.6 G*	-0.4 Y	3.3 G*	1.4
Std Error	1.0	1.0	0.9	1.0	0.5
2009 Mean NCE Gain	0.7 G	-0.5 Y	-11.1 R*	3.1 G*	-1.6
Std Error	1.0	1.0	0.9	0.9	0.5
2010 Mean NCE Gain	-5.7 R*	2.8 G*	-8.6 R*	-2.0 R*	-3.3
Std Error	1.0	1.0	0.9	0.9	0.5
3-Yr-Avg. NCE Gain	-2.7 R*	2.6 G*	-6.7 R*	1.5 G*	-1.2
Std Error	0.6	0.6	0.5	0.5	0.2
Estimated School Mean NCE Scores					
Grade	5	6	7	8	
District Base Year (2007)	50.0	50.0	50.0	50.0	
2007 Mean	56.2	54.2	54.5	59.7	
2008 Mean	56.9	61.8	53.8	57.8	
2009 Mean	52.5	56.4	50.7	56.9	
2010 Mean	49.5	55.3	47.8	48.7	

	G* - Estimated mean NCE gain is above the growth standard by at least 1 standard error.
	G* - Estimated mean NCE gain is equal to or greater than growth standard but by less than 1 standard error.
	Y - Estimated mean NCE gain is below the growth standard by 1 standard error or less.
	R - Estimated mean NCE gain is more than 1 standard error below the growth standard but by 2 standard errors or less.
	R* - Estimated mean NCE gain is below the growth standard by more than 2 standard errors.

Source: SAS® EVAAS® for K–12 content Copyright ©2011, SAS Institute Inc., Cary, NC, USA, All Rights Reserved. Used with permission.

Estimated School Mean NCE Scores) provides information on the mean achievement level of students. Generally, color-coding is used to indicate the significance of the results based on a growth standard that is determined by policymakers. Overall, this school value-added report provides aggregate-level results for each building in the system and is designed to help answer an essential question: How much growth was produced grade level by grade level across your school? Look at the report above to answer questions about ABC Middle School's value-added results for mathematics.

1. Which grade level has the highest mean achievement level in 2010? The lowest?
2. Which grade level produced the most growth in math in 2010? The least?
3. In terms of student gains, how well did the math program of this school perform as a whole in 2010?

Through your review of the report, you should have determined that sixth-grade students had the highest mean achievement level of 55.3 Normal Curve Equivalents (NCEs) and that seventh-grade students had the lowest mean achievement level of 47.8 NCEs. In terms of growth, this report indicates that in 2010 the sixth-grade students had the highest gains (mean NCE gain of 2.8), and the seventh-grade students experienced the least growth (mean gain of –8.6 NCEs). Overall in 2010, the math program, with the exception of Grade 6, did not perform as well as expected; aggregate student gains have declined each year over the last 3 years.

Pause to Practice

After reviewing the school value-added report for ABC Middle School can you

- Determine how the mean gain for eighth-grade mathematics in 2009 was calculated?
- Determine if the school's three-year average in Grade 5 exceeded the state's growth expectation for that same period?
- Determine if the gains made by sixth-grade students in 2010 were at, below, or above the expected mean gain?

Refer to Chapter 4 to assist you. Answers are provided at the end of this chapter.

As we have noted, the outputs generated from value-added analysis vary based on the analytics used and how the outputs are displayed. For example, the Value-Added Research Center (VARC) produces annual school-level value-added estimates for Wisconsin public schools, using scatter plots to depict the relative relationship between attainment (percentage proficient) and student growth (value-added data) in reading and math compared to all schools in the system. Figure 5.3 depicts an example of these school-level reports.

Now that you understand the primary aggregate-level school value-added report, the next step is to produce a Focus on My Building matrix for your school.

Concept 2: Produce a Focus on My Building Matrix to Assess Current Results

You met Tina Thomas-Manning, principal of Blendon Middle School, in Chapter 2. Tina later moved from Blendon Middle School to become the principal of Hannah Ashton Middle School in Reynoldsburg, Ohio. After spending two academic years at her new assignment, she became increasingly concerned about her fifth-grade math results. While 83.9% of her fifth-grade students had passing scores in reading, only 74.2% of them passed math. The math interventions she and her staff had put in place seemed to be making little difference. When her value-added reports were posted, she was surprised to see that her fifth-grade students' math gains far exceeded those same students' gains in reading. This was a revelation. Despite relatively low math performance, student growth in math was high: This meant that the work she and her staff had done over the past two years to adjust the academic schedule, introduce progress monitoring, and intervene through flexible grouping strategies was actually paying off. This kind of information is immediately apparent through the construction of a Focus on My Building matrix.

The Focus on My Building matrix is designed to plot achievement and value-added growth on the same grid to provide a more comprehensive view of school performance. The analysis at the building level can be done in exactly the same way as the analysis at the district level described in Chapter 4. A leadership team of building administrators and teachers is assembled, and building-level value-added and achievement information is examined. So instead of using district-level value-added and achievement information, the building-level team focuses its attention on building-level data. Beyond

Figure 5.3 Wisconsin Value-Added Comparison Report

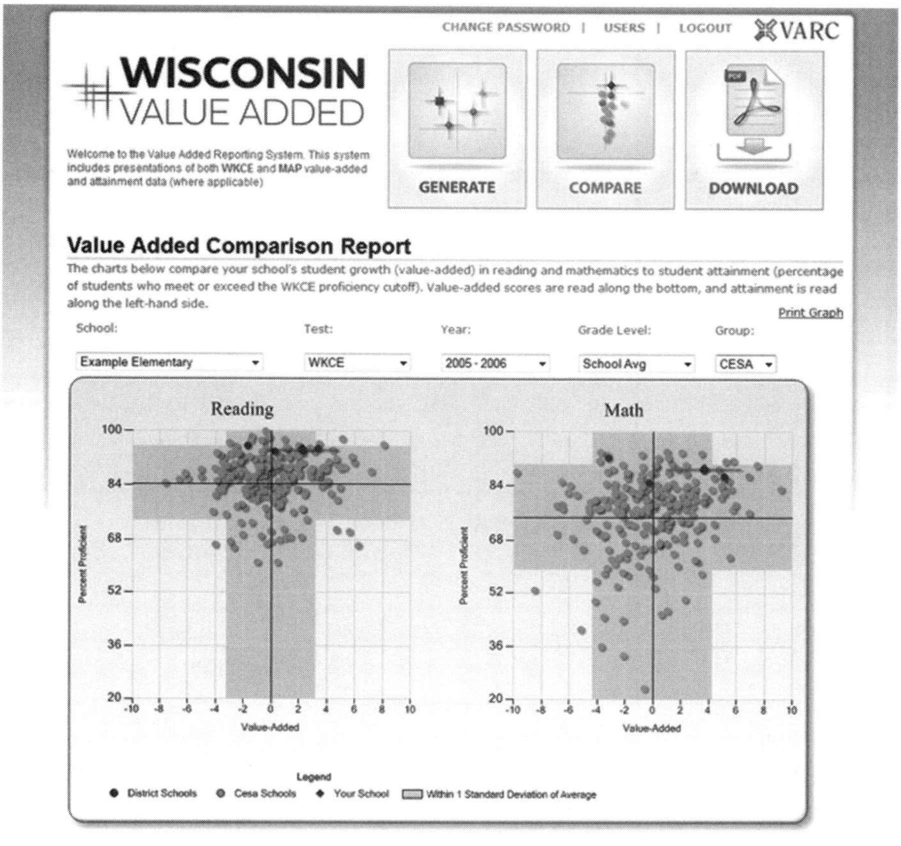
CHANGE PASSWORD | USERS | LOGOUT
VARC
WISCONSIN
VALUE ADDED
Welcome to the Value Added Reporting System. This system includes presentations of both WKCE and MAP value-added and attainment data (where applicable)
GENERATE
COMPARE
DOWNLOAD
Value Added Comparison Report
The charts below compare your school's student growth (value-added) in reading and mathematics to student attainment (percentage of students who meet or exceed the WKCE proficiency cutoff). Value-added scores are read along the bottom, and attainment is read along the left-hand side.
Print Graph
School:
Test:
Year:
Grade Level:
Group:
Example Elementary
WKCE
2005 - 2006
School Avg
CESA
Reading
Math
Percent Proficient
Value-Added
Legend
District Schools
Cesa Schools
Your School
Within 1 Standard Deviation of Average

Source: Value-Added Research Center (VARC), University of Wisconsin.

that difference, the work of the building-level team is exactly the same as the work of the district-level team.

Examining Aggregate-Level Data

An example of a middle school matrix is presented in Figure 5.4. The Focus on My Building matrix can be done exactly like the district-level matrix in Chapter 4, but other scales can also be used on the *x*- and *y*-axis. In Figure 5.4, the matrix is completed based on how each program area would rank in terms of its mean achievement level (*y*-axis) and mean student gains (*x*-axis). Q1 in this matrix refers to the lowest or first quintile of the state distribution of students, and Q5 refers to the highest or fifth quintile of the state distribution of students. A program area in the first quintile is in the bottom 20% of the state, and a fifth quintile program area is in the top 20% of the state.

Figure 5.4 Focus on My Building Matrix

Achievement Quintile (↑ Highest)	Q1	Q2	Q3	Q4	Q5
Q5					6th Math 8th Math 7th Science 6th Social St.
Q4	7th Math	5th Math 5th Science 8th Science	5th Reading 8th Reading 5th Social St.	6th Reading 6th Science	
Q3	7th Social St.				
Q2		7th Reading			
Q1				8th Social St.	
2009-2010	Progress Quintile				→ Highest

Just as in the district-level analysis, the team will find its greatest aggregate-level strengths in the top right-hand corner, its greatest challenges in the bottom left-hand corner, its high achievement and low growth program areas in the top-left, and its low achievement and high growth areas in the bottom-right.

You can see that this particular middle school has a very strong sixth-grade program and a relatively poor seventh-grade program, with the exception of seventh-grade science, which produced very strong results.

Concept 3: Examine Disaggregated Data to Determine Strengths and Challenges

The next step for the building team is to examine its disaggregated data to look for other kinds of patterns. Let's return to Hannah Ashton

Middle School, where principal Tina Thomas-Manning recognized a disparity in her math and reading achievement and growth data. Her students in fifth-grade reading had high achievement scores and low value-added gains. Her students in fifth-grade math had low achievement scores and high value-added gains. So her fifth-grade value-added scores were telling an entirely different story than her fifth-grade achievement scores. Then Tina asked the next questions.

- What were the patterns of growth for different student groups?
- Were there patterns within grades and across subjects?
- Were there patterns across grades and within subjects?

Along with her team, Tina turned to the disaggregate information available in her value-added reports. In Figure 5.5, you see the fifth-grade diagnostic reports that helped Tina uncover an important pattern in her results. The reports displayed in Figure 5.5 are produced by SAS and are available to districts through the EVAAS services of SAS Institute, Inc.

To help you interpret this diagnostic information, you may want to return to Chapter 4 to review the corresponding section that concerns diagnostic reports.

Recall that the darkest-grey bars in the two graphic representations above represent the most recent subgroups of fifth-grade students in Tina's school. In each report, the dark bar on the far left represents the students in her school whose achievement level would be in the bottom 20% of the pool or state. Similarly, the dark bar on the far right of each graph represents the students in her school whose achievement level would place them in the top 20% of the pool or state. The other three dark-shaded bars represent students in the other three quintile-based subgroups. The lighter-grey bars in each graph represent prior cohorts of students in the same categories. The thick horizontal line in each graph represents the expected progress level for each student subgroup. The dark and light bars that stretch below the thick line represent student subgroups that on average experienced less than expected progress. The dark and light bars above the thick line represent student subgroups that on average experienced more than expected progress. In all cases, the further above or below the thick line the more pronounced the growth above or below the expected level.

Tina's team reviewed the reports and quickly detected patterns evidenced in their results. Relative to the reading growth, they saw the overall magnitude of growth across all student groups was less than it was with prior cohorts. In addition, the highest and lowest

Figure 5.5 School Diagnostic Report (Reading and Math)

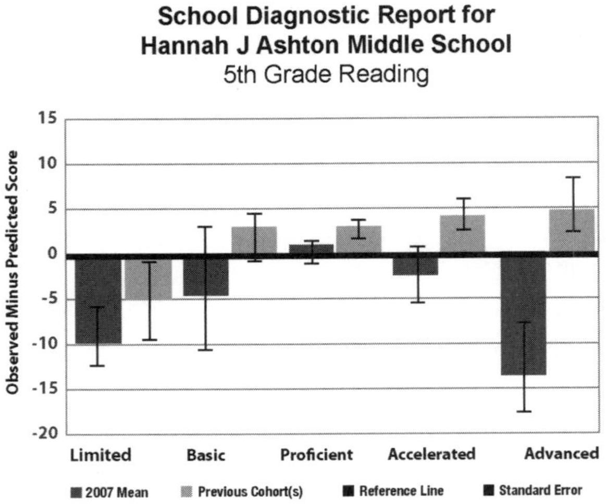
School Diagnostic Report for
Hannah J Ashton Middle School
5th Grade Reading
Observed Minus Predicted Score
15
10
5
0
-5
-10
-15
-20
Limited
Basic
Proficient
Accelerated
Advanced
2007 Mean
Previous Cohort(s)
Reference Line
Standard Error

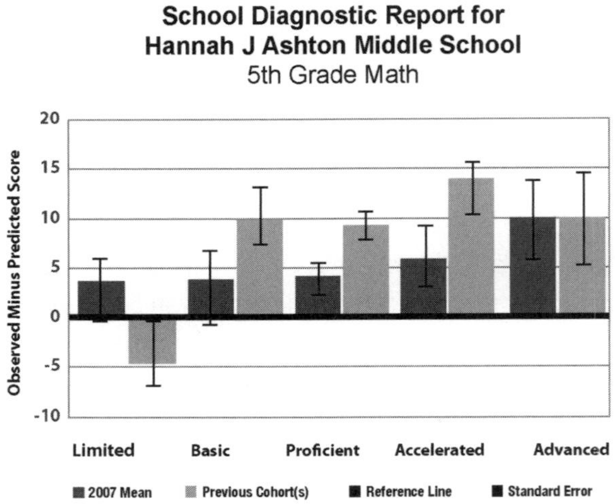
School Diagnostic Report for
Hannah J Ashton Middle School
5th Grade Math
Observed Minus Predicted Score
20
15
10
5
0
-5
-10
Limited
Basic
Proficient
Accelerated
Advanced
2007 Mean
Previous Cohort(s)
Reference Line
Standard Error

Source: SAS® EVAAS® for K–12 content Copyright ©2011, SAS Institute Inc., Cary, NC, USA, All Rights Reserved. Used with permission.

achieving subgroups were experiencing much less than expected growth. Only students in the middle were experiencing expected levels of growth. This news was alarming, but it provided real clues as to where the fifth-grade teachers needed to focus their attention to improve student reading gains.

In mathematics, the team was pleased to see an entirely different picture. They were producing expected or more than expected growth with each of their student subgroups. Collectively, they believed their comprehensive intervention efforts were paying off.

Regardless of the reporting mechanisms available to you, disaggregated building-level information is essential in helping you understand what is happening and why. This information increases your capacity to leverage your strengths and identify and address your challenges.

Summary

In buildings, such as those led by Bobby Moore and Tina Thomas-Manning, the use of data has become integral to the school's culture. They collect and review data routinely over the course of the entire school year to assess the effectiveness of their programs, to recognize their strengths, and to address their challenges. They actively provide time for teachers to respond to data and to engage teachers in the professional development they need to hone their analytic skills to productively use value-added information.

In this chapter, we concentrated on building your skills to interpret building-level reports and using that information to construct a Focus on My Building matrix to find patterns in disaggregated data. This matrix is useful for school leadership teams to understand the relationships between progress and achievement and determine those subjects and grades in which strengths and challenges exist. This stage of inquiry establishes the groundwork for the next level of analysis—the diagnostic work that is required to determine which student groups are benefiting most and least from the current instructional program. In the next chapter, we focus on teacher-level value-added reporting and how the BFK•Focus process is used to stimulate dialogue among teachers as they uncover areas of strength and challenge for their teams to address.

Pause to Practice Answers

After reviewing the school value-added report for ABC Middle School:

Determine how the mean gain for eighth grade in 2009 mathematics was calculated.

The mean gain of 3.1 was determined by subtracting the 2008 mean NCE score of 53.8 from the 2009 mean NCE score of 56.9.

Determine if the school's three-year average in Grade 5 exceeded the state's growth expectation for that same period.

ABC Middle School achieved a 3-year average gain of -2.7 NCEs. The state's expectation for growth is 0.0. Thus, the school did not exceed the state's expectations.

Determine if the gains made by sixth-grade students in 2010 were at, below, or above the expected mean gain.

The gains made by sixth-grade students in 2010 were above (2.8) the expected mean gain. Above, in this case, is indicated by the G (green in color-coded charts) that follows the mean gain score.*

Action Steps and Reflection Questions

Action Step: Make copies of all of the building-level reports (or display on a screen if possible) that you have available for your data analysis team.

Action Step: Assemble your data analysis team and devote at least two hours to analyzing your school-level data.

- Have you included educators from the different departments and grade levels?
- Have you included teachers who have value-added information available and those who may not? Consider the role of lower elementary, art, music, and physical education teachers, as well as the role of counselors and support persons.
- Does your data analysis team have the tools and resources it needs to be successful in assessing the current results and determining strengths and challenges? You might want to revisit Chapters 1 through 4 to make sure you've introduced everyone to value-added analysis and that they understand how it fits in a school improvement context.

Action Step: Produce a Focus on My Building matrix.

- What were the patterns of effectiveness across different grades and subjects?
- What are the strongest grade and subject programs?
- What grade and subject programs present the biggest challenges?
- Are there any vertical subject-based patterns?
- Are there any horizontal grade-level patterns?

Action Step: Uncover vertical and horizontal patterns in disaggregated data.

- What were the patterns of effectiveness relative to student subgroups?
- Are there any subject-based patterns across grade levels?
- Are there any grade-based patterns across subject areas?
- Are there any patterns that cut across grade levels and subject areas?

Hands-on Resource Guide for Teachers and Leaders

- Focus on My Building Matrix: Template

Figure 5.6 Focus on My Building Matrix: Template

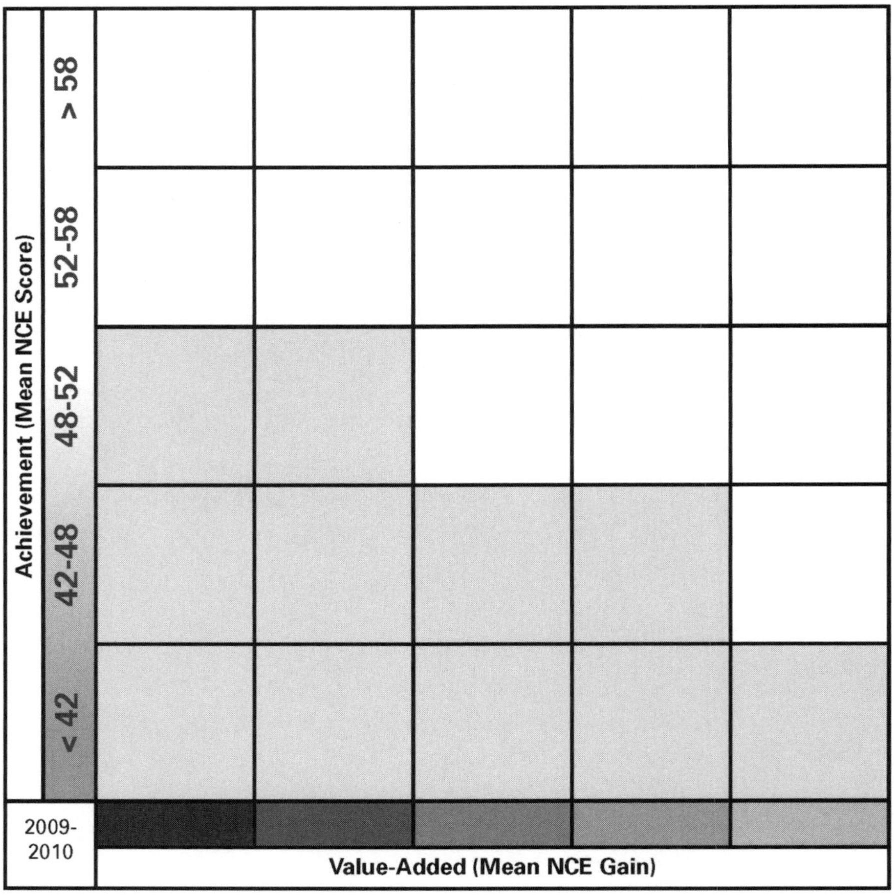
Achievement (Mean NCE Score)
> 58
52-58
48-52
42-48
< 42
2009-2010
Value-Added (Mean NCE Gain)

6

Step II

Assess Teacher-Level Value-Added Reports to Determine Strengths and Challenges

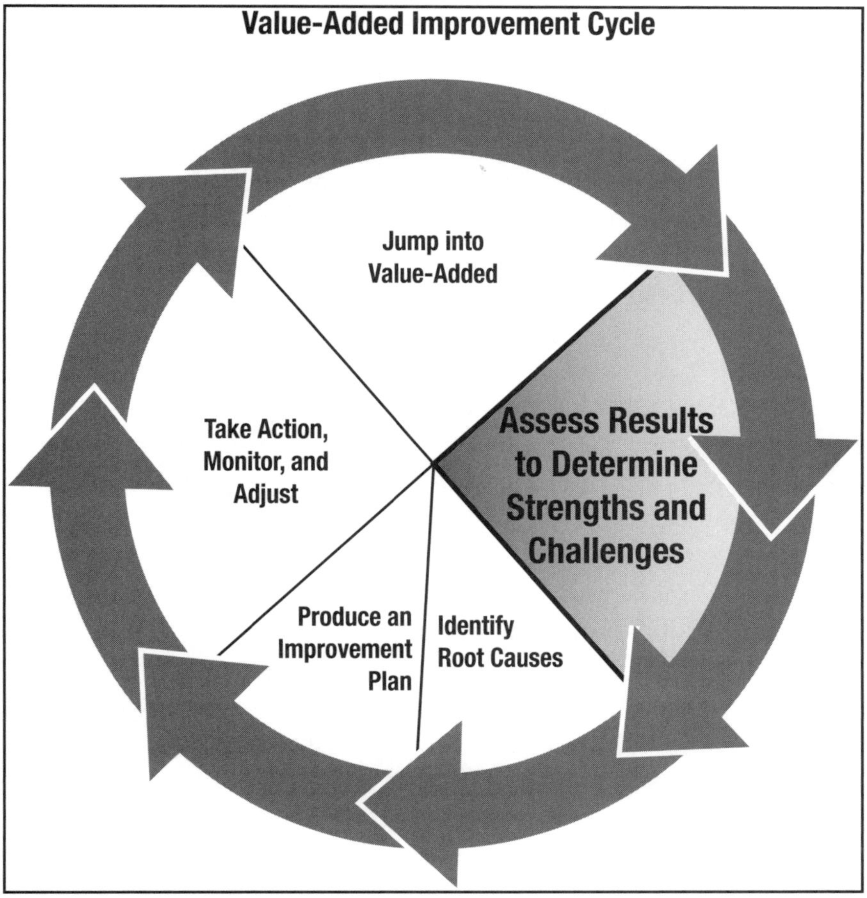
Value-Added Improvement Cycle
Jump into Value-Added
Assess Results to Determine Strengths and Challenges
Identify Root Causes
Produce an Improvement Plan
Take Action, Monitor, and Adjust

Source: © 2011, Battelle for Kids.

Chapter 6 Core Concepts

1. Teacher-level information is actionable.
2. Teacher-level value-added information must be handled with sensitivity.
3. Teacher and student attribution is necessary for accurate reporting.
4. Teacher-level analysis reflects what teachers do.
5. Collaborative teacher-level analysis focuses on uncovering improvement priorities.

Overview: Teacher-Level Value-Added Reports

The interest in and demand for teacher-level value-added reporting has exploded in recent years as national attention has been focused on teacher quality. As a direct result of the Obama administration's Race to the Top incentive program (RttT), teachers across the country from Atlanta, Georgia, to Los Angeles, California, are now provided with a measure of their effects based on the growth their students have made. In several places across the country, classroom teachers currently receive teacher-level analyses of their students' growth. Teachers in Tennessee, for example, have had teacher-level information available since 1993, and in Houston, Texas, teachers have received reports since 2007.

> Teacher-level value-added analysis is the most sensitive of all the value-added analysis that is available, but in terms of improvement this information is critical.

Teacher-level value-added analysis is important because it allows teachers to see how they differ in terms of the student results they produce in each of the subject areas they teach. This is the most sensitive of all the value-added analysis that is available, but in terms of improvement this information is critical. Teacher-level value-added data are also a key component of new teacher evaluation designs under RttT and a significant data source for strategic compensation decisions. Since this book has concentrated on the use of value-added analysis to establish improvement priorities and inform problem solving, we will not be delving into these other uses of value-added data. We will instead keep our focus on how the advent of teacher-level value-added information has the potential to promote meaningful change in student achievement, advance school culture, and shed new light on teacher practice. By highlighting a pilot project that was designed to deliver teacher-level value-added reports and related professional development to a consortium of Ohio school districts, we bring you a close-up view of a large-scale deployment of teacher-level reporting and the lessons learned along the way. You also will be exposed to some examples of teacher-level reports and stories about teachers who have been recipients of these reports.

Whereas teacher-level reporting is an important feedback mechanism for individual teachers, these reports are equally valuable as tools to uncover improvement priorities. The teacher level is where the most powerful discussions unfold about teaching and learning as colleagues use achievement and progress data to determine strengths they can leverage as well as challenges they must address. In the latter part of this chapter we move from the individual to the teacher-team level to put a spotlight on the final layer of our Focus on the System process. In doing so, we work through the protocol for using progress and achievement data to determine strengths and challenges.

Chapter 6 is the final chapter that explores the second step of the value-added improvement cycle, Assess Results to Determine Strengths and Challenges.

Concept 1: Teacher-Level Information Is Actionable

Educators have long understood that if changes in our American education system are to occur, they need to happen at the classroom level, where teachers interact with students on a daily basis. It is almost redundant to say that what teachers do matters most; of course, what teachers do matters. In fact, our education system depends on well-trained and well-supported teachers to meet the increasing demands of our rapidly changing society. Historically, teachers have most often been supported through various forms of professional development to help them develop their craft as well as teacher evaluation systems designed to provide them with feedback about their instruction. What has not been available to teachers is a measure of their own efficacy. How are teachers to gauge their own impact without fair and reliable measures that point to the change they produced in their students? With the availability of teacher-level value-added reporting, we now have a feedback mechanism that is grounded in statistical estimates of a teacher's contribution to student growth rather than relying solely on inputs, such as observational checklists to assess teacher quality. Given the opportunity, teachers who are provided with value-added reports can gain new insights into the impact they are making. Using the process described in this chapter and Chapter 7, teachers can identify improvements to accelerate student learning.

> Teachers can and do respond to value-added information in ways that positively change outcomes for their students.

Melanie is a teacher who had the opportunity to receive teacher-level value-added reports. As a fourth-grade teacher in a suburban middle school, she observed that her value-added results were very strong in mathematics but considerably weaker in reading, especially for her average students. This surprised Melanie, who considered herself to be a very competent teacher, and prompted her to consider what she could change about her instruction in reading to exact the same kind of results that she was getting in mathematics. Melanie visited other teachers' classrooms to see how they had organized their reading instruction. She investigated online tools for progress monitoring. She, along with her team, adopted some new instructional strategies that involved more frequent assessments of student fluency, comprehension, and writing. The team organized time so that all of the fourth-grade students were strategically and frequently regrouped. The value-added scores that Melanie and her team produced in reading increased steadily over time as a direct result of the initiatives undertaken by the fourth-grade team. Today, Melanie is an instructional coach who has helped improve the reading and math results in each of the buildings to which she has been assigned. Melanie's story gets to the heart of this chapter; that is, teachers can and do respond to value-added information in ways that positively change outcomes for their students.

Principles Guiding the Delivery of Teacher-Level Value-Added Reporting

- The teacher must be the catalyst of any real school-improvement initiative.
- Achievement and progress data are needed to create a complete picture of school and teacher effectiveness.
- When reliable diagnostic information about teacher effectiveness is provided to trained principals and teachers, it becomes the stimulus for sustainable continuous school improvement and subsequently higher student achievement.
- Educators must receive high-quality, targeted professional development to best understand and use this data to achieve the ultimate goal.

Anne is a sixth-grade mathematics teacher in a rural school district. Like Melanie, the teachers in Anne's school district have received teacher-level value-added information since 2007. At that time, a consortium of districts was formed by Battelle for Kids (BFK) to launch Teachers Connecting Achievement and Progress (T-CAP), a three-year pilot initiative that resulted in teacher-level value-added analysis in Grades 3 through 8 for over forty Ohio school districts. Since T-CAP began as a pilot initiative, independent researchers have conducted numerous interviews with teachers and administrators who shared their ideas about the promise of and concerns surrounding teacher-level reporting. Overall, the interviewees pointed to the importance of sustained dialogue and professional development around the appropriate interpretation and use of value-added data at the classroom level, the impact that these data may have on school cultures, and the power they could have regarding instructional and management decision making. The themes that emerged from the interviews are captured below. Take time to read the comments that the teacher respondents made about the impact that teacher-level value-added information is making. Some of their statements point out that the information provided to them was well received and helped them to consider their practices in new ways. But other teachers who were interviewed remained unclear about how to appropriately interpret the value-added information.

These teachers' comments serve as both a positive and cautionary signal for administrators who enter into this arena. The fact that teachers expressed their enthusiasm about the usefulness of these data is encouraging. The caution is that this does not happen accidentally. School leaders must take away the fear and mystery that surrounds the value-added metric and instead provide teachers with solid professional development and support in a safe, caring environment.

Teacher Voices: Themes From Teacher Interviews About Value-Added

Positive Outlook. Most teachers interviewed were positive about the current and future utility of teacher-level value-added reports.

> "To me, this adds that extra layer of information. You really need to not be satisfied with the fact that our kids are just being successful; we need to really make sure they are being as absolutely successful as they can be because of what we're doing."

Accelerated Understanding of Value-Added. Many of the teachers indicated that their exposure to and use of value-added data was limited before the teacher-level value-added data were made available, even though their districts had received value-added results at the building, subject, and grade level for years.

> "Aside from the (teacher) reports, I'm not really sure whether there is any value-added data that we use. I know my principal shares it with us, but that (teacher) report is mine."

Equitable Resources Concerns. Multiple teachers expressed concerns regarding the fairness of teacher-level value-added scores, based on the different levels of resources and instructional support provided to teachers.

> "I'm not sure it (teacher-level value-added reports) gives an accurate picture. I worry about the poor fifth-grade teacher whose scores are compared to mine, when I have an hour of reading intervention every day, and she has 30 minutes and the same number of kids."

Value-Added Information Is Being Used. Multiple teachers could describe specific strategies or modifications to instruction based, at least partly, on value-added data.

> "We have altered scheduling to match teachers whose delivery system is consistent with how students learn. We're waiting to see whether this was a good decision or a bad decision."

> "It is interesting because my teaching partner did better with the high end (students), and I did better with the low end (students). I had the same group of students for two years and maybe was more attuned to that lower set of kids. Maybe my instruction was too slow or it was too basic for my higher kids. What I thought about for this year was, what can I do differently?"

Making Strategic Connections. Teachers expressed a need for specific strategies connected to various value-added results.

> "I had no growth with my middle kids; they stayed the same. I want to know what caused that. Is it literary text, is

it nonfiction, or is it vocabulary? That's the stuff I need—not just that I didn't reach the middle kids. In what areas did I not reach the middle kids? I'm not sure that's possible with value-added."

Additional Information Is Needed. Several teachers indicated that value-added data does not provide specific information about student skills that can help drive instruction. For example, the data are not broken out by indicator or strand, such as literary text for reading.

"If I'm having trouble with the low kids, tell me where I'm having trouble with the low kids. Why would I do extra lessons on vocabulary if everyone were doing well in vocabulary?"

Time to Learn. Some teachers expressed frustration with both time to process and overall understanding of value-added information in general and teacher-level value-added reports in particular.

"The biggest (reason) why I probably don't use it (value-added information) enough is the time. When my principal sat down with me, he made time during the school day, which was really helpful."

"I think some of it (why teachers aren't using their value-added information) would be just finding the time and really sitting down, evaluating, and really thinking about it."

Data Analysis. Teachers stressed the increased reliance on various types of data to make instructional decisions.

"I think it's brought a lot of kids to the forefront."

Concept 2: Teacher-Level Value-Added Information Must Be Handled With Sensitivity

The introduction of teacher-level value-added analysis can have a palpable effect on the very culture of the school. These data represent a fundamental shift in how teacher quality is measured and teachers are judged.

> The introduction of teacher-level value-added data can have a palpable effect on the very culture of the school.

Historically, teachers have been judged not on the effects of their instruction but on measures such as classroom management, student engagement, lesson planning, and delivery. The prevailing cultural norms that generally view teachers as interchangeable and equal contributors to the school community are challenged when student outcomes are the key defining variables. Schools in which classroom data are shared regularly and openly for the purpose of examining one's practice and to elicit strategies for improvement are rare. Even more unlikely is finding instances where teachers are routinely recognized for their measurable contribution to student growth. Instead, historically egalitarian school cultures support environments where each teacher is, in effect, an independent contractor assigned to deliver instruction in the manner that fits best.

The introduction of teacher-level reports begins to differentiate teachers using quantifiable measures that have the potential to be made public. Consequently, it should be no surprise that teachers and teacher unions have raised concerns about the validity of value-added measures and have expressed vehement objections over the use of such metrics to define teacher quality. Unless school leaders, teachers, and the public are well informed about what value-added results are saying and how they should and should not be used, concerns and recalcitrance will be heightened. The axiom "people are down on what they are not up on" applies well here.

Another point to consider is that the current national attention on compensation reform may have the unintended effect of dampening teacher's enthusiasm about the use of teacher-level reports for diagnostic purposes and thereby creating additional deployment challenges. Recent public debates and initiatives, such as the RttT competition, have galvanized state and local union officials as well as opinion and policy leaders to speak out about the use of student performance measures to evaluate, reward, and compensate teachers. Teachers are concerned that value-added information will be used to judge them unfairly and in ways that may affect their assignments, tenure, and potentially their compensation expectations. They can point to the ranking of teachers in the Los Angeles Unified School District by the *Los Angeles Times* (Felch, Song, & Smith, 2010) as evidence that information about teacher effects will be made public and used to forward political agendas rather than to help teachers improve their practice.

Additionally, educators fear that value-added information at the teacher level will foster competition for rewards and recognition (Harris, 2011). In schools where collaboration is viewed as a positive and necessary component of a healthy school climate, it is unknown if teacher-level reports will have the unintended consequence of reinforcing competition and efforts to suppress open sharing of teacher-level value-added report information. It is conceivable that if a direct link is made between compensation reform and value-added results, more teachers will turn their attention away from the diagnostic potential of the teacher-level reports and focus only on evaluation and compensation issues.

How do you deal with the cultural and political pressures that surround the use of value-added metrics? First, school leaders must be aware of and responsive to the new demands and responsibilities that teacher-level value-added information brings. Leaders need to be sensitive to the impact teacher reports have on a teacher's sense of worth. Principals need to find appropriate ways to share and discuss each teacher's report discreetly. But we also encourage leaders to build an environment where teacher-level data can be routinely shared openly among colleagues in a manner that is safe and respectful. Finally, leaders need to help teachers respond to the information they receive by guiding them towards reflective thinking and taking productive action.

> We also encourage leaders to build an environment where teacher-level data can be routinely shared openly among colleagues in a manner that is safe and respectful.

We conclude this section by emphasizing that these responsibilities do not fall solely on one or two persons in an organization. Individuals at each level of the organization have a responsibility when it comes to the successful deployment of teacher-level reports. Based on the lessons learned during the course of our work, here is our best thinking about what leaders and teachers can do to assure that teacher-level value-added data are accessible, that they are handled with sensitivity, and that their usefulness is maximized:

What District Leaders Should Do

- Assure that building leaders and principals know how to interpret value-added reports.
- Provide tangible action steps and expectations for principals to follow for preparing and sharing value-added data with teachers.
- Encourage principals to use value-added information as part of their school improvement planning.

- Provide principals with concrete instructional methods and strategies they can share with their teachers.
- Develop a communications plan and be prepared to explain the results with your school board and media.

What Principals Should Do

- Share this information sooner rather than later. Data-literate principals tend to routinely promote a culture of sharing information. When administrators don't view themselves as proficient in value-added analysis, or where there is no established culture to support data-based discussions, they tend not to share or discuss teacher-level value-added reports with their teachers at any length. Conversely, principals who routinely explore data with staff and have confidence in interpreting value-added reports tend to more often engage their staff in productive, data-driven discussions.
- Use this information to
  - pair teachers with students with whom they are most successful,
  - partner teachers with other teachers who may complement their strengths,
  - determine program efficacy,
  - identify students who are not making sufficient progress and design intervention plans,
  - customize professional development based on student growth patterns, and
  - stimulate discussions during the school year about ongoing measures of student growth.
- Focus attention on teachers who remain at either end of the performance spectrum. That is, teachers who consistently score significantly below or above growth expectations over time should get the attention of administrators.
- Leverage information about effective teaching.
  - Begin a conversation about teacher quality with staff. Talk about the importance of everyone growing in their ability to provide the kind of instruction that causes students to progress. Value-added information becomes an invaluable source of information once this reality is accepted.
  - Identify and leverage highly effective teachers. The easiest and least intrusive way to leverage highly effective teachers is to simply tell them that they are extraordinarily good at

what they do. By communicating genuine admiration and appreciation directly to these teachers, principals will be repaid exponentially. High-quality teachers will work to make themselves and their peers better and are often willing to take on critical leadership roles within the building.
  - Spend at least part of your valuable time in the classrooms of highly effective teachers. In these classrooms, you will learn a lot about leadership—great teachers are great classroom leaders—and a lot about what it is that effective teachers do to be effective.
- Build the case for a balanced assessment system and provide the tools to accomplish it. This includes both the appropriate use of sound formative assessment strategies and summative assessments to measure student progress being made both during the school year and over time, respectively.
- Provide teachers with
  - opportunities for ongoing collaboration among teachers to discuss data and actionable strategies,
  - tools and examples of what to do next based on various patterns in value-added scores,
  - opportunities to determine strategies to implement with students in each quintile,
  - information about what highly effective teachers do to promote student academic growth,
  - opportunities to openly address specific questions related to the fairness of teacher-level value-added analysis and school policies that may augment or detract from maximized results,
  - multiple examples of how to use other data, such as item analysis, in combination with value-added information to establish priorities, to determine root causes, and to plan strategically, and
  - examples of effective teacher/ and classroom data systems, such as data notebooks that track progress of individual students.

What Teachers Should Do

- Use value-added data to determine strengths and challenges.
- Engage in purposeful collaborations with fellow teachers to discuss value-added information and actionable strategies.

- Locate highly effective teachers and observe what they do to promote student academic growth.
- Use formative data to monitor student progress and guide practice during the course of the school year.

It is our hope that these suggestions will help you to better access, utilize, and act upon your value-added information.

Concept 3: Teacher and Student Attribution Is Necessary for Accurate Reporting

Early on in our work to get teachers value-added information in the hands of teachers, we discovered that state and district data systems do not capture the multiple, complex relationships found in today's schools. In a given year, classroom variables change constantly. Students move into and out of the classroom. Teachers regroup or reassign students to other classrooms for instructional reasons. Teachers leave or are reassigned. Some students may receive additional instructional support or enrichment. As a result, students often receive instruction from multiple teachers. Thus, data collected from districts by the state's department of education at the beginning of the school year often did not reflect end-of-school-year teacher and/or student status. For instance, changes made to teacher or student assignments were not up to date. Finally, descriptive information about teachers, such as years of experience and educational background, were often erroneous or incomplete.

In all, we discovered that the source data that are typically available generally fail to capture necessary data elements:

- Course scheduling
- Student regrouping
- Student and teacher mobility
- Co-teaching/shared instruction
- Mapping course to tested subject

To address these data inadequacies, we realized that an annual data verification process is needed. In other words, in order to generate teacher-level value-added reports the test data needed to be *cleaned* and students linked to the appropriate teachers. Once the data are prepared, they can then be delivered to statistical experts for analysis and subsequent report generation. Below is the linkage process we use to assist schools to verify data for teacher-level reporting. The process serves to accurately identify which teacher taught what subject to a particular student and to capture the percentage of instructional time spent between the teacher and student.

A key lesson learned from the pilot on teacher-level reporting was that to produce teacher-level reports that accurately capture a teacher's influence on a student, it is critical to identify which teacher taught what subject to a particular student and to capture the percentage of instructional time spent between the teacher and student.

Five Important Steps for Successful Teacher Verification of Student Results

1. Collect the Best Data Available. Begin with the most accurate sources of data, including
   - student course,
   - teacher assignment data,
   - principal assignment data, and
   - translation or association of course codes to state tests.
2. Create Secure Access. Create secure user accounts using identifying information to validate user access. Local knowledge of the data is important, not only to ensure accurate linking but also to establish transparency and buy-in from stakeholders.
3. Establish Administrator Setup and Review Periods. Allow the principal or administrative designee to quickly establish the teaching assignments as they occur throughout the year.
4. Engage Teachers in the Verification Process. By understanding the data that go into the system, teachers have more confidence and trust that the information accurately reflects their classroom and students. Therefore, teachers need to
   - review and modify course rosters by adding or removing students,
   - indicate class membership by setting student entry and exit dates (for mobility),
   - set the percentage of instructional time, and
   - submit assignments for review and approval.
5. Complete the Administrator Validation and Approval Process. Once teachers have made their corrections, the principal reviews the data and adjusts for errors and omissions.

It is important to note that when teachers become involved in verifying the students they teach, they are more likely to anticipate and trust the results.

Although this process may seem somewhat onerous, our experience is that by instituting technical support measures such as step-by-step how-to manuals, annual regional or district-wide face-to-face training sessions, phone support, or an online support ticketing system, the process can be streamlined and is relatively painless. It is important to note that when teachers become involved in verifying the students they teach, they are more likely to anticipate and trust the results.

Concept 4: Teacher-Level Value-Added Analysis Reflects What Teachers Do

Now that we have shared the lessons learned through providing teachers with individual reports, let us turn to the actual reports. We have no doubt that the look and sophistication of value-added reporting mechanisms will rapidly advance as demand for this information increases. As was mentioned in Chapters 4 and 5, even now, teacher-level reports look different across various school districts and states depending on the entity that produces the outputs. For instance, the Value-Added Research Center (VARC) produces annual teacher-level reports for New York City, Los Angeles Unified School District, Chicago Public Schools, and Wisconsin schools. In Tennessee, teachers access annual teacher-level reports that are produced by SAS and made available through a secure website.

Value-added reports generally include two distinct pieces of information. The first aspect of a typical report provides an estimate of teacher effectiveness. This measure represents the relative growth that a teacher produces over a school year. The effects tend to be categorized by level to represent if the effects were below, at, or above the expected growth estimate for that grade and subject in that year as compared to the average growth produced by the average teacher in the pool to which the teacher is being compared.

Another crucial feature of a strong value-added report is disaggregated information about the growth patterns of student groups. Figure 6.1 depicts information about the growth patterns of students assigned to an algebra teacher. This information, similar to a report produced by SAS and available to districts through the Education Value-Added Assessment System (EVAAS services of

Figure 6.1 Teacher-Level Value-Added Report

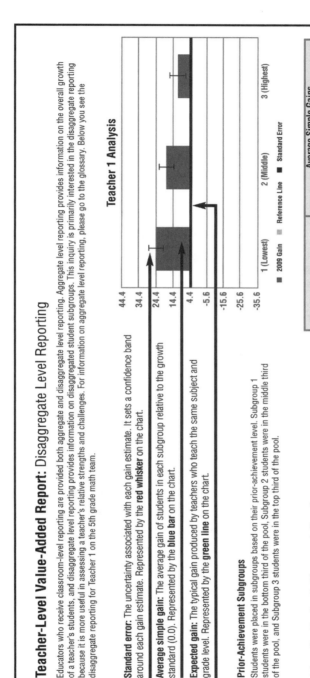

Teacher-Level Value-Added Report: Disaggregate Level Reporting

Educators who receive classroom-level reporting are provided both aggregate and disaggregate level reporting. Aggregate level reporting provides information on the overall growth of a teacher's students, and disaggregate level reporting provides information on disaggregated student subgroups. This inquiry is primarily interested in the disaggregate reporting because it is more useful in assessing a teacher's relative strengths and challenges. For information on aggregate level reporting, please go to the glossary. Below you see the disaggregate reporting for Teacher 1 on the 5th grade math team.

Standard error: The uncertainty associated with each gain estimate. It sets a confidence band around each gain estimate. Represented by the **red whisker** on the chart.

Average simple gain: The average gain of students in each subgroup relative to the growth standard (0.0). Represented by the **blue bar** on the chart.

Expected gain: The typical gain produced by teachers who teach the same subject and grade level. Represented by the **green line** on the chart.

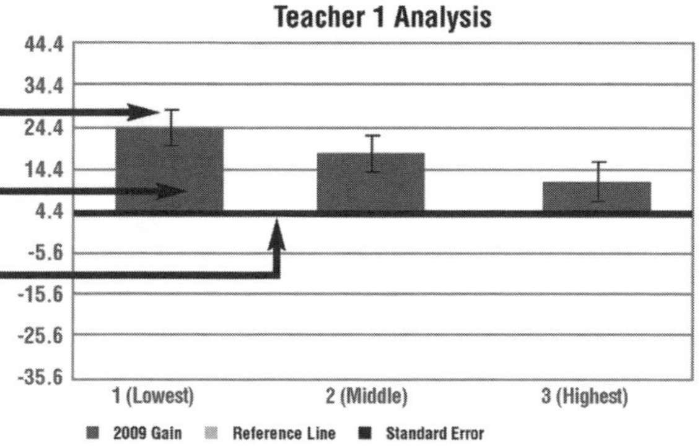

Teacher 1 Analysis
44.4
34.4
24.4
14.4
4.4
-5.6
-15.6
-25.6
-35.6
1 (Lowest)
2 (Middle)
3 (Highest)
2009 Gain
Reference Line
Standard Error

Prior-Achievement Subgroups

Students were placed in subgroups based on their prior-achievement level. Subgroup 1 students were in the bottom third of the pool, Subgroup 2 students were in the middle third of the pool, and Subgroup 3 students were in the top third of the pool.

Interpreting Teacher 1's Disaggregate Report

Teacher 1 had eight students in each subgroup. Students in Subgroup 1 scored, on average, 25.0 NCEs above the growth standard and almost 21 NCEs above the district's reference gain (25.0 - 4.4) for 5th grade math students. Similarly, Subgroup 2 scored, on average, 19.2 NCEs above the growth standard and almost 15 NCEs above the reference gain. Subgroup 3 scored 11.9 NCE's above the growth standard and more than 7 NCEs above the reference gain. All of these gains were significant at one standard error. Teacher 1 produced exemplary results, especially with students in the first two subgroups.

		Average Simple Gains		
		Prior-Achievement Subgroups		
		1 (Lowest)	2 (Middle)	3 (Highest)
Year				
2009	Ref Gain	4.4	4.4	4.4
	Avg Gain	25.0	19.2	11.9
	Std Error	3.4	6.4	6.1
	Nr of Students	8	8	8

Source: SAS® EVAAS® for K–12 content Copyright ©2011, SAS Institute Inc., Cary, NC, USA, All Rights Reserved. Used with permission.

SAS Institute, Inc.), helps teachers determine the groups with whom they have been most successful. You can see that this teacher has been most successful with the lowest performing students—those students who have been assigned to the lowest tertile group, or the lowest 33% of students, based on their prior performance. We can also conclude that all three groups of students are growing more than expected. This information gives teachers the opportunity to reflect on the success—or lack thereof—they had with the strategies employed with their students during the previous school year.

Another example of a teacher-level report, used by the New York City Department of Education and produced by VARC, is shown in Figure 6.2.

This teacher value-added data report features a teacher rating, which is based on the percentile group into which the teacher's value-added scores fall. On the top of the first page, teachers are provided with sample data to assist them to interpret the bottom portion of the report. The sample report includes a clear description about how the value-added scores were generated using a predicted mean calculation.

On the bottom half of this report, teacher Hunt Russet is provided information about his current value-added scores and a four-year average compared to other teachers who have similar years of experience and who teach the same subject. The gains Hunt achieved were in the 89th percentile for 2008 to 2009, and four-year average results place him in the 84th percentile. Hunt was given an above-average rating for both the current year and the four-year average.

In Figure 6.3, Hunt's report shows valuable disaggregate information about the gains that were made by student subgroups.

From the first graph, Hunt can determine if and how his students' growth varies by three performance groups, or tertiles, based on their prior academic performance. This report reveals that students who were assigned to the top, middle, and lowest performance groups all had above-average growth.

Hunt, along with all New York City teachers, also receives value-added information disaggregated by gender, English language learner (ELL), and special education status. The subreport indicates that Hunt is producing average growth with his ELL students. He is producing above-expected levels of growth with his males, females, and students with special needs and thus has been given an above-average rating in each of those categories.

Figure 6.2 New York City Teacher Data Report

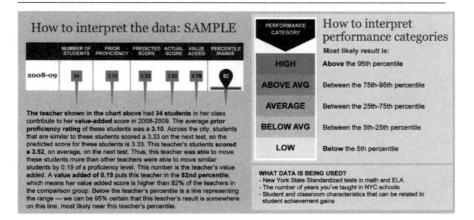

Big Apple 123
6th Grade
Years Teaching in NYC: More Than 3 Years

NYC Department of Education TEACHER DATA REPORT
MATH HUNT RUSSET

Teacher Data Reports–a different perspective

Every day, you and your principal see the impact you have on your students' learning in multiple ways, including student work, student feedback, and classroom observation.

Sometimes, though, it's helpful to understand how your impact compares with teachers across the city. **Teacher Data Reports provide that different perspective.**

How to interpret the data: SAMPLE

	NUMBER OF STUDENTS	PRIOR PROFICIENCY	PREDICTED SCORE	ACTUAL SCORE	VALUE ADDED	PERCENTILE /RANGE
2008-09	34	3.10	3.33	3.52	0.19	82

The teacher shown in the chart above had **34 students** in her class contribute to her **value-added** score in 2008-2009. The average **prior proficiency rating** of these students was a **3.10**. Across the city, students that are similar to these students scored a 3.33 on the next test, so the predicted score for these students is 3.33. This teacher's students **scored a 3.52**, on average, on the next test. Thus, this teacher was able to move these students more than other teachers were able to move similar students by 0.19 of a proficiency level. This number is the teacher's value added. A **value added of 0.19** puts this teacher in the **82nd percentile**, which means her value added score is higher than 82% of the teachers in the comparison group. Below the teacher's percentile is a line representing the range — we can be 95% certain that this teacher's result is somewhere on this line, most likely near this teacher's percentile.

How to interpret performance categories

PERFORMANCE CATEGORY	Most likely result is:
HIGH	**Above** the 95th percentile
ABOVE AVG	Between the 75th-95th percentile
AVERAGE	Between the 25th-75th percentile
BELOW AVG	Between the 5th-25th percentile
LOW	**Below** the 5th percentile

WHAT DATA IS BEING USED?
- New York State Standardized tests in math and ELA
- The number of years you've taught in NYC schools
- Student and classroom characteristics that can be related to student achievement gains

How do my results compare to other teachers?

The chart below shows how your results compared to those of other teachers who teach the same grade, the same subject area and have a similar amount of experience.

My Results	NUMBER OF STUDENTS	PRIOR PROFICIENCY	PREDICTED SCORE	ACTUAL SCORE	VALUE ADDED	MY PERCENTILE / (RANGE) 0% 25% 50% 75% 100%	PERFORMANCE CATEGORY
2008-2009	75	3.59	3.61	3.82	**0.21**	89	ABOVE AVG
Last 4 Years	295	3.32	3.27	3.43	**0.15**	84	ABOVE AVG

LEARN MORE! Learn more about how to read this report at: Interpret the Report

Source: Used with permission from New York City Department of Education.

Figure 6.3 New York City Teacher Data Report: Subgroups

Big Apple 123
6th Grade
Years Teaching in NYC: More Than 3 Years

NYC Department of Education TEACHER DATA REPORT
MATH HUNT RUSSET

My results with student subgroups

The chart below shows your results with subgroups of students, compared to other teachers in the **same grade, subject area**, and who have been teaching for more than 3 years. When available, the chart uses up to four years of data. Are there specific groups with which you could improve?

	NUMBER OF STUDENTS	PRIOR PROFICIENCY	PREDICTED SCORE	ACTUAL SCORE	VALUE ADDED	MY PERCENTILE / (RANGE) 0% 25% 50% 75% 100%	PERFORMANCE CATEGORY
By Prior **City-wide** Student Achievement Levels							
Top 3rd	82	3.96	3.62	3.74	**0.12**	78	ABOVE AVG
Middle 3rd	139	3.33	3.32	3.48	**0.16**	84	ABOVE AVG
Lowest 3rd	74	2.61	2.80	2.99	**0.19**	88	ABOVE AVG
By Gender							
Male	98	3.32	3.22	3.36	**0.14**	81	ABOVE AVG
Female	197	3.32	3.30	3.46	**0.16**	85	ABOVE AVG
Other Groups							
ELL	13	3.01	3.03	3.06	**0.04**	60	AVERAGE
Special Ed.	72	3.11	3.05	3.20	**0.15**	84	ABOVE AVG

HAVE QUESTIONS? The Teacher Data Toolkit answers frequently asked teacher questions and has resources to help you understand key concepts.

Source: Used with permission from New York City Department of Education.

Pause to Practice

Take a few minutes to review Hunt's value-added reports. What observations can you make about

1. the differences among students grouped by prior performance,
2. the differences between males and females, and
3. the rate of growth being made by special education students as compared to students in the lowest performance group?

Hunt Russet is fortunate because his value-added reports include the disaggregate information necessary to help him determine his strengths and areas of challenge. Value-added reports that simply rank teachers by their effects have no diagnostic value for teachers or administrators. The exemplars in Figures 6.2 and 6.3 include both overall teacher ratings and information about the growth the teacher has produced among different groups of students. Once teachers become familiar with these reports, they can begin to identify any patterns that signal areas of strength that can then be leveraged to address areas of challenge.

Note that Hunt Russet's value-added report indicated that his instruction tends to meet the needs of all of his students, as he is performing at above average or average with all of his students. However, while he is producing above-average growth with his top, middle, and lowest students as well as above-average growth with his males, females, and special education students, he is promoting average growth with his ELL students. With this understanding, he may be prompted to consider how he and his teacher-team members can determine the root causes for this discrepancy so that they can implement some well-informed strategies designed to accelerate the growth of ELL students. This phase of the Focus on the System process is described in the next chapter.

We conclude this section with an invitation to read Jessica Cynkar's own story about her journey with her value-added results. Jessica, a sixth-grade teacher, exemplifies how teachers can effectively use disaggregate-level data to modify and enhance the effectiveness of their practice.

Jessica: One Teacher's Value-Added Journey

Jessica Cynkar, sixth-grade teacher, Olentangy Local School District, Ohio

The first teacher-level value-added report I received was for the 2007 to 2008 school year. Honestly, I wasn't that surprised. It seemed to fit with everything that I had learned about the reports and teaching in general; it followed a bell curve, and I was clearly teaching to the middle. However, after reflecting, I knew that I didn't challenge my high kids enough, and I was disappointed that my low kids actually had the lowest growth. Overall, my teaching was average. I had to ask myself was I okay being just average. During the next school year, I began to think about the different groups of students I was teaching. As a result,

I incorporated more differentiated lessons into my teaching and gave students a choice—not as to what they were learning—but how they learned the material.

At first glance, my next year's results were disappointing. The (disaggregate) bars at all levels were on the 0 line or very, very close to average. However, when I compared these results to the previous year, my data showed that I was doing better. What did that tell me? The gap between my high and low kids was definitely starting to shrink. Wasn't that what I wanted? I was beginning to do something right.

The actual satisfaction came during the 2009 to 2010 school year. For the first time, all of my (disaggregate) bars were above the line. My teacher effect score was finally positive for the low, the middle, and the high kids! I had worked hard incorporating formative assessments into my instruction and really tried to help students who didn't understand the material to finally *get it*. If someone asked me what I did to get here I would say two things: First, my goal was to assure that all students had a voice everyday: everyone talked and participated. It was a free zone where mistakes were welcome and encouraged because they were learning experiences. Second, our English department worked together to come up with common definitions of key terms and concepts. We shared and created lessons that matched what we were supposed to teach, and we began to write common assessment questions. By doing this, I learned about and accepted my strengths and weaknesses as a teacher as well as the strengths and weaknesses of the other people in my department. This really helped me to see that not only did everyone have room to grow but they also had room to teach everyone. In the end, we are all there to help the kids grow and succeed. Am I where I want to be? Not yet, but I am definitely moving in the right direction!

Concept 5: Collaborative Teacher-Level Analysis Focuses on Uncovering Improvement Priorities

Now that we have discussed the essence and importance of teacher-level reporting, we move on to what to do with teacher-level reports by exploring the third level of the Focus on the System process. We began at the system or district level, proceeded to the building level, and now focus on a pivotal component of the process: the teacher-team level.

Collectively, the members of teams have greater potential to produce measurable improvement than do individual teachers. Teams include more points of view and strengths, are more likely to solve difficult problems, and have a higher level of accountability than do individuals. Think of improvement as dancing with a bear: You can't quit when you get tired! The source of fuel for this difficult work is mutual support that is readily available on a team but is less available for individuals who are going it alone. But we also recognize that although teams can study data, make decisions, and support change processes, it is individual teachers who act. Real improvement hinges on whether individual teachers can change the dynamics in individual classrooms. So focusing attention on the team in no way reduces the responsibility that individual teachers have for improving their practice. Teams only make this difficult process more productive.

Team-level data are, in fact, simply the aggregate of teacher data. Value-added reports and achievement data that are provided by the grade and subject level are especially useful for grade- and department-level teams to determine patterns and identify improvement priorities. Members of teacher teams can also share individual teacher-level value-added and classroom achievement data results with each other. For instance, teachers like Hunt Russet can share their individual teacher-level value-added results with peers publicly or can privately contribute the knowledge gained from their own reports to the team's improvement work.

Putting Together a Team

This may seem obvious, but the most important thing to consider in deciding who is on what team is that team members must share something important in common. This commonality could be a group of students the teachers share, such as the students on an interdisciplinary middle school team; it could be a common curriculum, such as the four core subject areas that define the work of self-contained teachers on a grade-level team; or even a single common discipline, such as a team of high school teachers who all teach math. Ultimately, the people on the team must be tied together in one or more important ways, or some teachers' data won't connect with other teachers' data.

> The data analysis process works best if someone external to the team acts as facilitator.

Regardless of the makeup of the team, the data analysis process works best if someone external to the team acts as facilitator, especially the first time or two that a team moves through this process. An external facilitator who has no face to save with the group can suggest meeting structures, pose questions, and direct attention in ways that someone on the team likely cannot.

Examining Aggregate-Level Data

Once the team is assembled, the analysis process is essentially the same as for the other two levels of the system. The only difference for a teacher team is that it is dealing with a smaller whole than the teams at the other two levels of the system. But even given this smaller whole, it is essential that teacher teams go through this process. The reason for this is simple. One of the most important early findings from value-added research is that there is at least as much variability among results within a school as across schools (Aaronson, Barrow, & Sander, 2007; Rivkin, Hanushek, & Kain, 2005; and Rockoff, 2004). This means that the strengths and challenges that characterize one team within a school are likely very different from the strengths and challenges that characterize another team. This is why the analysis cannot stop at the school level; real teachers, like real students, have different skills, likes, dislikes, and needs. Analysis at the teacher-team level is necessary to uncover and address these differences.

The simplest way for a teacher team to begin its analysis is to examine those parts of the school-level matrix that relate to the team. Suppose, for example, that a particular middle school has both self-contained and disciplinary-based classrooms. All of the fifth-grade teachers are self-contained so they form a grade-level team. In Figure 6.4 we see the same middle school's focus matrix that was examined in Chapter 5. In this matrix, however, the fifth-grade results are highlighted.

As the fifth-grade team examines its results on the matrix, it is apparent that the team is having little problem with the achievement level of its students. The average achievement level in all four fifth-grade subject areas is above average. In terms of growth, however, students are somewhere between the 20th and 40th percentiles in math and science and somewhere between the 40th and 60th percentiles in both reading and social studies. Clearly the disaggregated growth data will be important to examine next.

Examining Disaggregate Data

The process for examining the fifth-grade team's disaggregate-level data is also very similar to the disaggregate analysis at the other two levels, described in Chapters 4 and 5. The only difference is that the fifth-grade team has no vertical data to examine. In Figure 6.5, the fifth-grade disaggregated data are displayed. The reports displayed

Figure 6.4 Focus on My Building Matrix

Achievement Quintile (Highest ↑)	Q1	Q2	Q3	Q4	Q5
Q5					6th Math 8th Math 7th Science 6th Social St.
Q4	7th Math	5th Math 5th Science 8th Science	5th Reading 8th Reading 5th Social St.	6th Reading 6th Science	
Q3	7th Social St.				
Q2		7th Reading			
Q1				8th Social St.	
2009-2010	Q1	Q2	Q3	Q4	Q5
	Progress Quintile →				Highest

in Figure 6.5 are produced by SAS and are available to districts through the EVAAS services of SAS Institute Inc.

In general, with the exception of math, the higher achieving students assigned to this team are experiencing more progress than their lower achieving peers. And in fifth-grade math, where the pattern is the opposite, lower achieving students are only making expected growth. So in terms of an area of strength, the team is generally producing adequate growth with its higher achieving students. With respect to this strength, however, the team must examine what is happening in math. High achievers have very poor growth in math.

In terms of disaggregate-level challenges, the team is doing poorly across the board with its lowest achievers. Even in math, where the lowest achieving students are experiencing more growth than their high achieving peers, they are still only experiencing expected levels of growth. Expected growth is not moving these

Figure 6.5 School Diagnostic Reports (Fifth Grade)

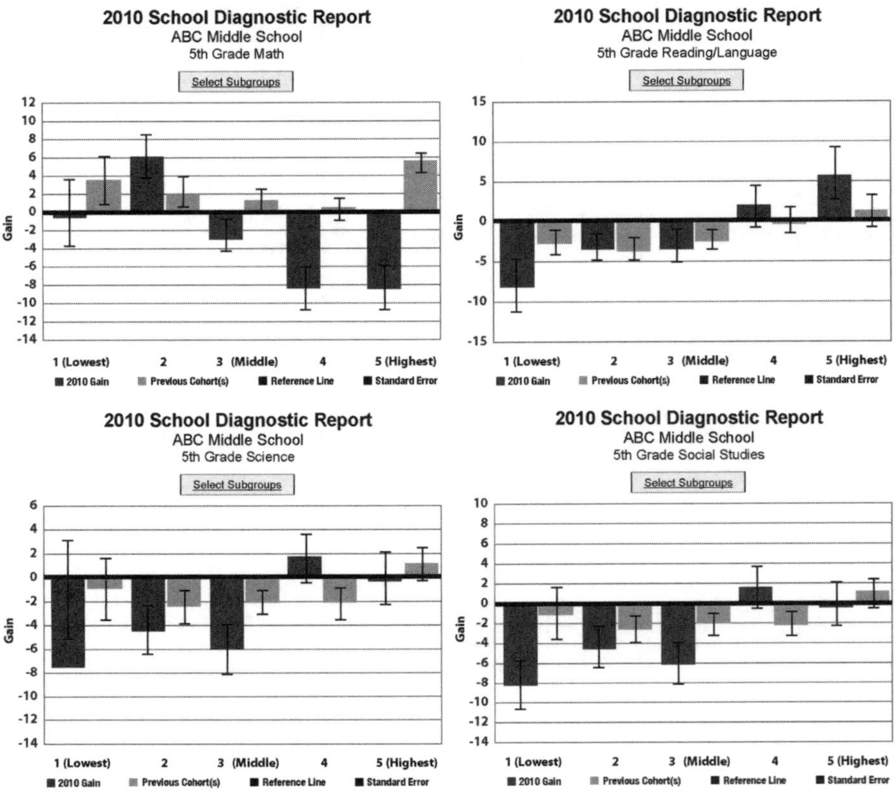
2010 School Diagnostic Report
ABC Middle School
5th Grade Math
Select Subgroups
Gain
12
10
8
6
4
2
0
-2
-4
-6
-8
-10
-12
-14
1 (Lowest)
2
3 (Middle)
4
5 (Highest)
2010 Gain
Previous Cohort(s)
Reference Line
Standard Error
2010 School Diagnostic Report
ABC Middle School
5th Grade Reading/Language
Select Subgroups
Gain
15
10
5
0
-5
-10
-15
1 (Lowest)
2
3 (Middle)
4
5 (Highest)
2010 Gain
Previous Cohort(s)
Reference Line
Standard Error
2010 School Diagnostic Report
ABC Middle School
5th Grade Science
Select Subgroups
Gain
6
4
2
0
-2
-4
-6
-8
-10
-12
-14
1 (Lowest)
2
3 (Middle)
4
5 (Highest)
2010 Gain
Previous Cohort(s)
Reference Line
Standard Error
2010 School Diagnostic Report
ABC Middle School
5th Grade Social Studies
Select Subgroups
Gain
10
8
6
4
2
0
-2
-4
-6
-8
-10
-12
-14
1 (Lowest)
2
3 (Middle)
4
5 (Highest)
2010 Gain
Previous Cohort(s)
Reference Line
Standard Error

students any closer to proficiency. With lower achieving students, we need to see more than expected growth every year if they are to catch up with their peers.

It is also interesting to note that even though the achievement level of the fifth-grade students is somewhat higher in reading and social studies, the growth patterns in these two subject areas are no better than in the other two subject areas. So in this case, the disaggregate growth data are telling a very different story than the aggregate-level achievement data.

Summary

The advent of teacher-level value-added reports is providing an increasing number of teachers and teacher teams with an opportunity to examine the impact of the learning environments they have constructed for their learners. This is powerful information that should be handled with sensitivity, as it will invariably impact your school's culture. Although the large-scale effects of teacher value-added reporting largely remain to be seen, the reaction that teachers have to this information is mainly up to school leaders. We have seen that providing professional development about report interpretation is a necessary but insufficient step toward helping educators use their results to inform instructional decisions. School leaders must actively and knowledgeably guide teacher teams to productive discourse and processes that perpetuate meaningful action. Once teacher teams have access to achievement and value-added information, the nature of collaborative conversations will change immeasurably.

The Focus on the System process that unfolds at the team level is potent. When teachers work together to complete the Focus on the Building matrix they are able to recognize patterns in the data that reveal areas of strength and challenge that prompt an obvious but vital question: Why did we produce these results?

Chapter 4 centered on the first two stages of the three-stage Focus on the System process at the district level, and in this chapter and Chapter 5 we explored the same process and how it plays out at the school and teacher-team levels. These stages use aggregate and disaggregate progress and achievement information to identify and prioritize strengths and challenges. In Chapter 7 we explore the third and final stage of the Focus on the System process to examine the *why*—the root causes for the results.

Pause to Practice Answers

Take a few minutes to review Hunt's value-added reports. What observations can you make about

1. the differences among students grouped by prior performance,

A: There is no difference among students grouped by prior performance. Students assigned to the highest, middle, and lowest performance categories based on prior achievement all demonstrated great growth (above average).

2. the differences between males and females,

A: Essentially, there is no discernible difference between males and females.

3. and the rate of growth being made by special education students as compared to students in the lowest performance group?

A: The growth for each group is *above average*. There is no discernible difference between the growth of special education students and the lowest performance group.

Action Steps and Reflection Questions

Action Step: Consider how you will handle teacher-level value-added reports.

- Will they be handed out in confidential one-on-one meetings?
- Will they be shared in a large staff meeting?
- Have you discussed how the data will be used with staff and colleagues?
- Have you allotted time for teachers to explore their reports and discuss their results with one another in a safe, supportive environment?

Action Step: Study your teacher-level report.

- Where are your strengths?
- Areas of challenge?
- What subgroups performed the best? Worst? Consider lower, middle, and higher achievers as well as ELLs, special education, and gender subgroups.

Action Step: As a team, explore your teacher-level disaggregate data.

- When you review the Focus on the Building matrix, where are your grade levels and subject areas? In the areas showing high growth and high achievement? High growth but low achievement? Low growth but high achievement? Or low growth and low achievement?
- As you lay out your various teacher-level reports, how did low achievers progress? Average achievers? High achievers?
- Among your team, where are the areas of strengths? Areas of challenge?

Hands-on Resource Guide for Teachers and Leaders

- Value-Added Report Investigation for Teacher-Level Reports (see Figure 6.6)

Figure 6.6 Value-Added Report Investigation for Teacher-Level Reports

Make sure you have paper copies of your teacher-level value-added reports available as you discuss the following questions individually or as a team:
Where are your strengths? List your strengths here:
In what areas are you facilitating expected growth? List areas of expected growth here:
In what areas are you facilitating less-than-expected growth? List areas of low growth here:
Where are your areas of high growth and high achievement? Consider how you might replicate those practices:
Where are your areas of high or low achievement but low growth? How might you ramp up your practices in these areas?

7

Steps III and IV

Identify Root Causes and Produce an Improvement Plan

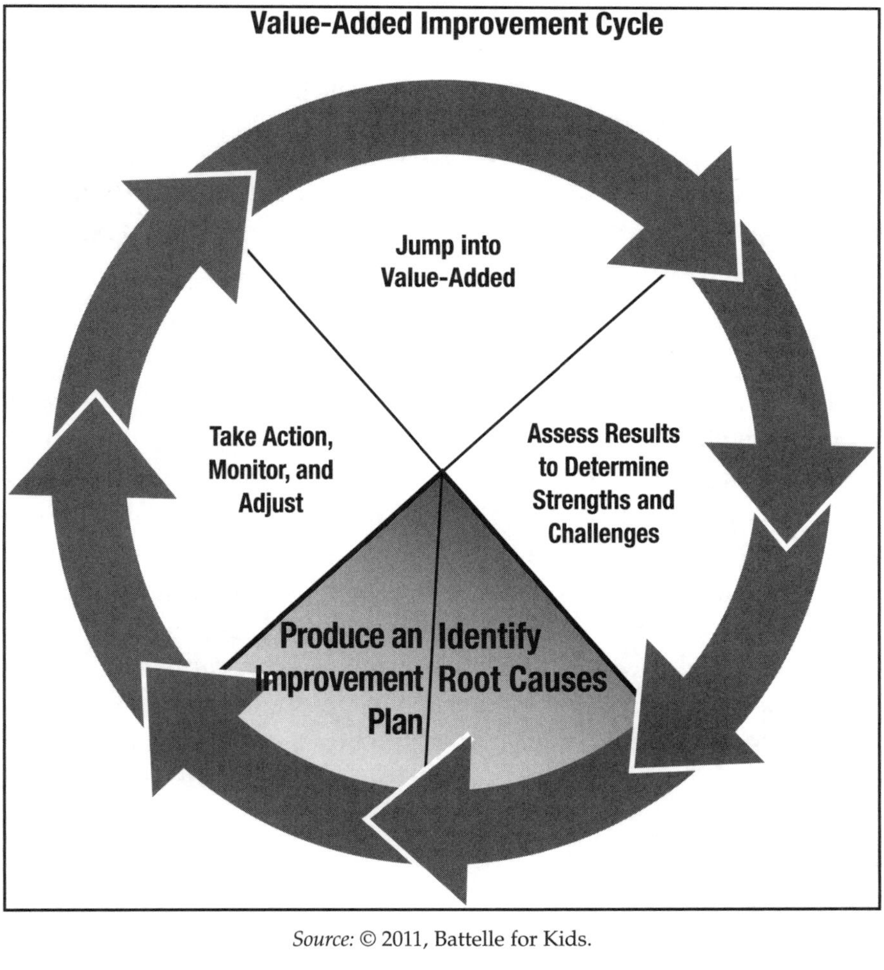

Value-Added Improvement Cycle
Jump into Value-Added
Assess Results to Determine Strengths and Challenges
Identify Root Causes
Produce an Improvement Plan
Take Action, Monitor, and Adjust

Source: © 2011, Battelle for Kids.

Chapter 7 Core Concepts

1. Root causes provide significant levers for improvement.
2. Root cause analysis is predicated on individuals taking personal responsibility for their current state.
3. It is essential to analyze a team's strengths.
4. A list of root causes must be pruned to retain only those that are principally responsible for a particular student outcome.
5. Produce a Strategic, Measurable, Attainable, Relevant, and Time Bound, or SMART, goal and an action plan to complete the Focus on the System process.

Overview: Identify Root Causes and Produce an Improvement Plan

Chapters 4, 5, and 6 were about how to use aggregate- and disaggregate-level progress and achievement information to identify and prioritize the strengths and challenges at each level of a school system. Once educators at each level have satisfactorily identified their highest leverage strengths and most significant challenges, the next step is to explore their root causes.

Why Examine Root Causes?

The primary reason for examining root causes is that they provide a significant lever for action. In recent years, educators have spent more time studying student performance data than ever, but studying data is not the same thing as taking action. The familiar phrase *analysis paralysis* aptly describes what all too often results from data analysis. This paralysis is produced by many sources. In many cases, student performance data, and especially achievement data, are equivocal. It is difficult to know whether the issues represented in the data arise from a team's instruction or from the instruction students received in prior years. Even when the data are less equivocal, there may be more challenges than a team is equipped to take on.

> Studying data is not the same thing as taking action.

To move past this paralysis toward action it is crucial that a team of educators (1) tackle a very short list of challenges and (2) explicitly explore why they are getting the results they have uncovered. If they do these two things there is a much greater likelihood that data exploration will lead to data-driven action. This step in the Focus on the System process is explicitly designed to lead teams toward action. Throughout this chapter we describe this phase of the process and how it actually unfolded with a team of fifth-grade teachers from the Houston Independent School District (HISD).

Concept 1: Root Causes Provide Significant Levers for Improvement

For our purposes, root causes are factors that tend to produce particular organizational outcomes—in this case, the highest leverage strengths and most significant challenges identified through the processes in Chapters 4, 5, and 6. By definition, root causes are factors over which educators have considerable influence. Root causes are not things, such as students' socioeconomic status or lack of parental support, because educators have little short-term influence over those factors.

The primary reason for uncovering and exploring root causes is that they provide significant levers for improvement. It stands to reason that if team members understand what they did to produce high-quality results, those same capacities can be leveraged to produce additional high-quality results. By the same token, if team members understand what they did to produce less-than-desirable outcomes, those practices can be modified or transformed to improve the quality of student learning and ultimately, their performance outcomes.

Concept 2: Root Cause Analysis Is Predicated on Individuals Taking Personal Responsibility for Their Current State

Perhaps the biggest difference between being an educator today and an educator twenty years ago is that in the past, educators were held accountable for what *they* did—lesson plans, graduate-level coursework, teaching performance, and so on. Today, they are held accountable for what their *students* do. This is not to say that student outcomes were unimportant twenty years ago, but without common assessments and value-added analysis, there was no way to use student outcomes to assess teacher quality. With the advent of annual state testing and value-added analysis it is now possible to reliably estimate the impact that teachers have on the academic gains of students. Given these metrics, it is now appropriate to hold educators accountable for the gains their students produce.

One important reason for taking educators through root cause analysis is that it forces them to grapple with the question of responsibility. Root cause analysis assumes that educators are responsible for both the good and the poor results that emerge from their classrooms. So with root cause analysis the question is always the same: What did I/we do that resulted in particular outcomes?

One important reason for taking educators through root cause analysis is that it forces them to grapple with the question of responsibility.

To practice *taking responsibility* it is important to begin a team's root cause analysis by examining an area of strength. There are two important reasons for starting here. First, educators are typically not reluctant to take responsibility for good outcomes. By exploring how their actions resulted in high-quality results, educators will be much more open to talking about how some of their actions may have resulted in lower quality results.

A second reason to begin with an area of strength is that teachers, and educators in general, pay too little attention to things that go well. Strengths are usually dismissed as "something we don't have to worry about." It is, in fact, essential that educators study the root causes of their strengths because these practices provide real examples of how high-quality outcomes are generated. The root causes of success can and should be leveraged to produce higher levels of success in other areas.

Concept 3: It is Essential to Analyze a Team's Strengths

A strength-based analysis begins with a cause and effect diagram called a fishbone. Dr. Kaoru Ishikawa, a Japanese quality control statistician, invented the fishbone diagram. The fishbone diagram is an analysis tool, often used in Total Quality Management (TQM) endeavors to provide a systematic way of looking at effects and the causes that create or contribute to those effects. A typical fishbone is illustrated in Figure 7.1.

To begin the analysis of an area of strength, the specific area of strength is written in the oval *head* of the fishbone. The large and small bones behind the head are used to write down the potential

Figure 7.1 Fishbone Diagram

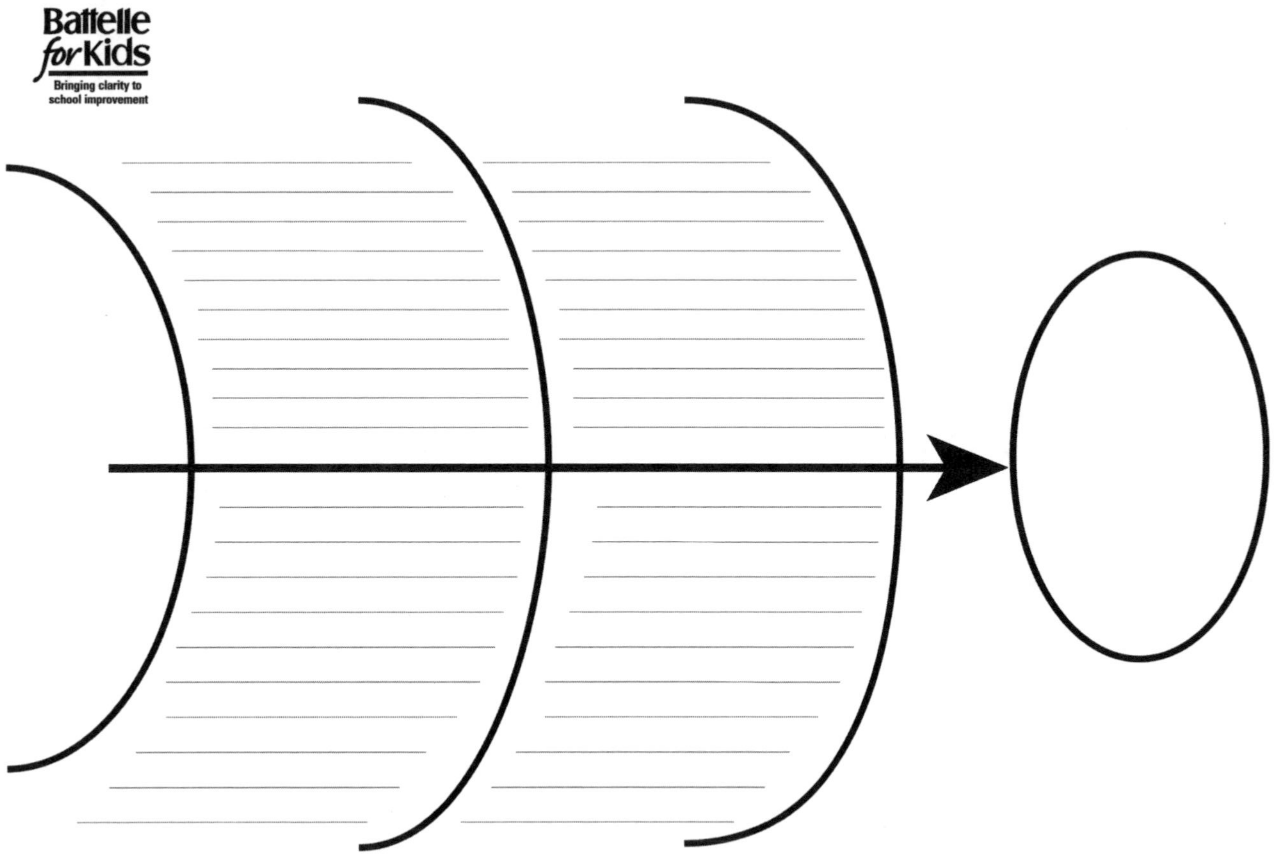
Battelle for Kids
Bringing clarity to school improvement

Source: © 2011, Battelle for Kids.

causes of the area of strength. Typically, the larger bones—the bold lines in the diagram—are used to signify large categories of causation. So for example, if this fishbone is focused on classroom outcomes, one large bone might be instruction, and another large bone might be assessment. Once these high-level categories are identified, subcategories are added underneath. So, under instruction we might list cooperative learning, differentiated instruction, whole group instruction, or learning centers as strategies that could be producing the identified area of strength.

In our work, when we facilitated groups using completely empty fishbones like the one in Figure 7.1, we were met with an uncomfortable silence. We realized that educators are typically not used to thinking about their practice in causal terms. To get things moving, we began to experiment with fishbones that already included some categories and subfactors. We made sure to leave empty spaces for participants to add additional factors, but fishbones with some meat on them seemed to work better than those that were completely blank. In Figure 7.2 you see an example of a classroom-level strength-based fishbone with some factors already added. The only caution with using this kind of fishbone is that the facilitator must really push to get the participants to add additional factors.

In practice then, a partially labeled fishbone is used to help educators identify root causes associated with a particular area of strength. Typically, we ask each individual on a classroom-level team to examine the fishbone one category at a time, beginning with the instructional factors. The core question is, Are there any instructional strategies your team is currently using that could reasonably be producing the identified area of strength? If there are additional strategies that could be producing your area of strength, add those factors in the blank spaces. After each person in the group does this individually, the group shares their results. Next, they come to consensus on the strategies that could reasonably be producing the identified area of strength.

This same process is then repeated with the other three categories. For each of these categories there are core questions:

- Is there some aspect of your curriculum or other systemic factors that could reasonably be producing the identified area of strength?
- Is there some aspect of how you assess your students that could reasonably be producing the identified area of strength?
- Is there some aspect associated with your development as a teacher that could reasonably be producing the identified area of strength?

Figure 7.2 Fishbone Diagram: Areas of Strength

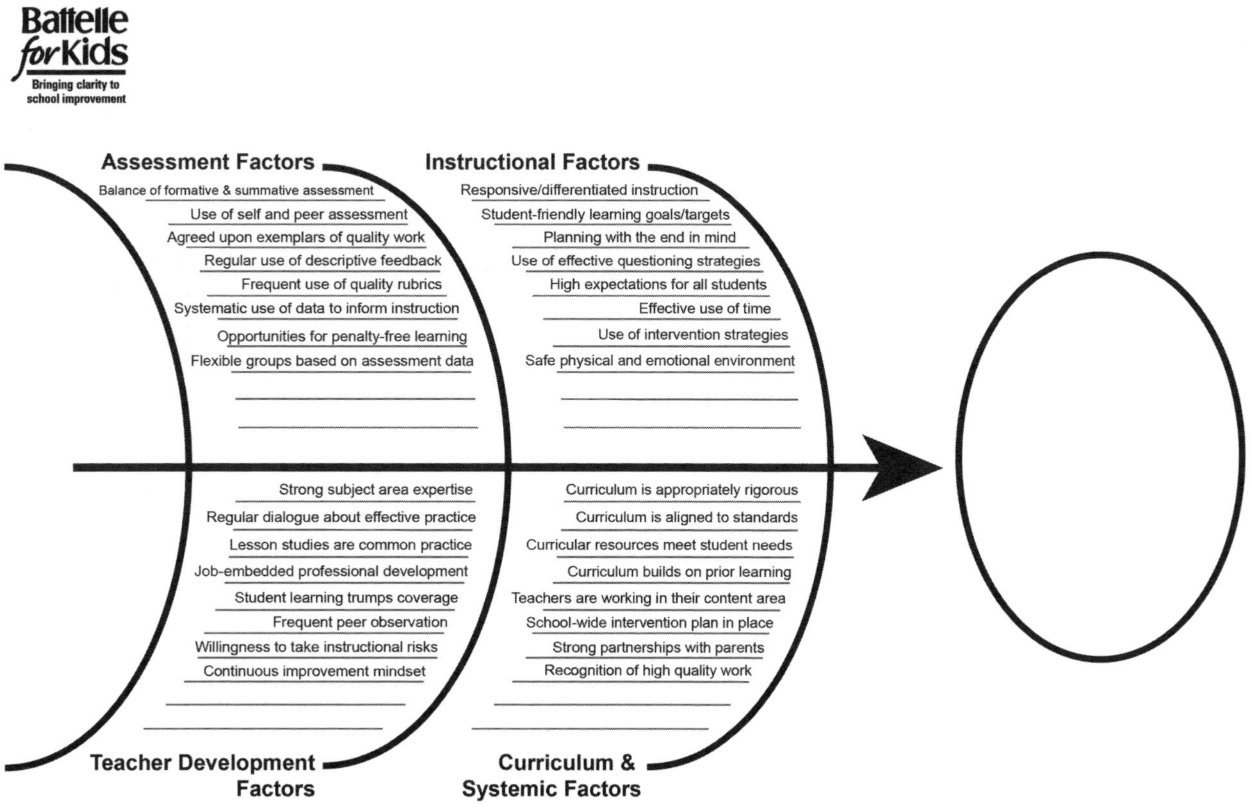
Battelle for Kids
Bringing clarity to school improvement
Assessment Factors
Balance of formative & summative assessment
Use of self and peer assessment
Agreed upon exemplars of quality work
Regular use of descriptive feedback
Frequent use of quality rubrics
Systematic use of data to inform instruction
Opportunities for penalty-free learning
Flexible groups based on assessment data
Instructional Factors
Responsive/differentiated instruction
Student-friendly learning goals/targets
Planning with the end in mind
Use of effective questioning strategies
High expectations for all students
Effective use of time
Use of intervention strategies
Safe physical and emotional environment
Strong subject area expertise
Regular dialogue about effective practice
Lesson studies are common practice
Job-embedded professional development
Student learning trumps coverage
Frequent peer observation
Willingness to take instructional risks
Continuous improvement mindset
Teacher Development Factors
Curriculum is appropriately rigorous
Curriculum is aligned to standards
Curricular resources meet student needs
Curriculum builds on prior learning
Teachers are working in their content area
School-wide intervention plan in place
Strong partnerships with parents
Recognition of high quality work
Curriculum & Systemic Factors

Source: © 2011, Battelle for Kids.

Concept 4: A List of Root Causes Must Be Pruned to Retain Only Those That Are Principally Responsible for a Particular Student Outcome

After each category had been addressed, the group revisits their final list of root causes and pares it down to include only those factors that the group can argue are principally responsible for the identified area of strength. For each root cause that is retained, the group should be able to cite evidence—either objective data or subjective experience—that supports the inclusion of that particular root cause. This final list, typically between two and four root causes, becomes the set of root causes for the identified area of strength.

Only after a concerted effort to probe an area of strength should the team begin to study its identified area of challenge. The process of probing for root causes in an area of challenge is exactly the same as the process described above, except that the fishbone is constructed around factors that produce challenges rather than strengths. An example of a classroom-level challenge fishbone is displayed in Figure 7.3.

But even as a team explores an area of challenge, team members must always remember that they have experience in producing high-quality results. This knowledge is essential in deciding how to address their area of challenge.

Concept 5: Produce a SMART Goal and an Action Plan to Complete the Focus on the System Process

To complete the Focus on the System process, a team uses its identified root causes, for both its area of strength and its area of challenge, and develops a SMART goal and action plan for how the team will address its core challenge. The first known use of this mnemonic device is attributed to George T. Doran in 1981. It was used in the context of project management as a means for evaluating the objectives or goals of an individual project. Most educators have had experience with writing SMART goals, but they will likely still need some coaching and support to produce a measurable goal that is both achievable and worthy of achievement. Figure 7.4 includes some additional details about constructing a SMART goal. A SMART goal is a goal that meets particular requirements for specificity as captured in the acronym SMART.

Figure 7.3 Fishbone Diagram: Areas of Challenge

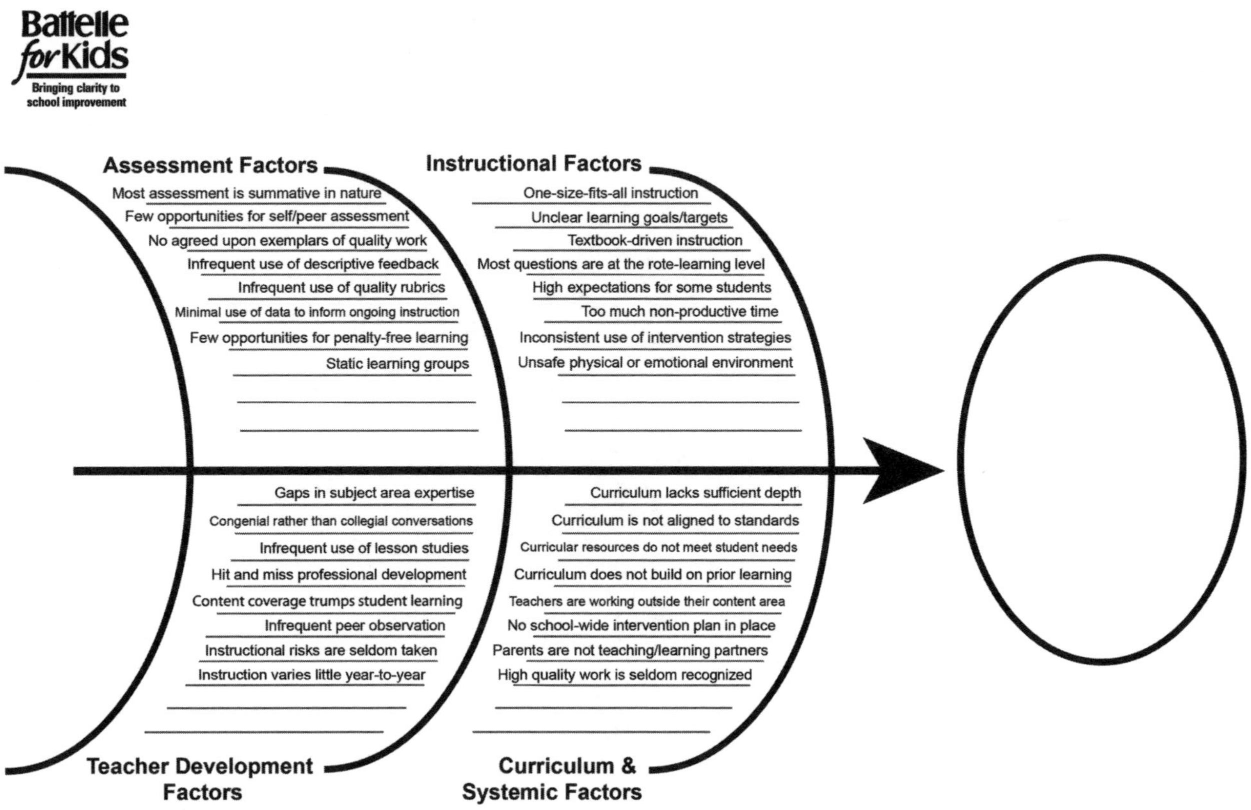
Battelle for Kids
Bringing clarity to school improvement
Assessment Factors
Most assessment is summative in nature
Few opportunities for self/peer assessment
No agreed upon exemplars of quality work
Infrequent use of descriptive feedback
Infrequent use of quality rubrics
Minimal use of data to inform ongoing instruction
Few opportunities for penalty-free learning
Static learning groups
Instructional Factors
One-size-fits-all instruction
Unclear learning goals/targets
Textbook-driven instruction
Most questions are at the rote-learning level
High expectations for some students
Too much non-productive time
Inconsistent use of intervention strategies
Unsafe physical or emotional environment
Gaps in subject area expertise
Congenial rather than collegial conversations
Infrequent use of lesson studies
Hit and miss professional development
Content coverage trumps student learning
Infrequent peer observation
Instructional risks are seldom taken
Instruction varies little year-to-year
Teacher Development Factors
Curriculum lacks sufficient depth
Curriculum is not aligned to standards
Curricular resources do not meet student needs
Curriculum does not build on prior learning
Teachers are working outside their content area
No school-wide intervention plan in place
Parents are not teaching/learning partners
High quality work is seldom recognized
Curriculum & Systemic Factors

Source: © 2011, Battelle for Kids.

Figure 7.4 SMART Goals

S	**Strategic:** A SMART goal is designed to improve both the short- and long-term effectiveness of your teaching team and your students' learning experience. It clearly states, in simple language, exactly what you want to accomplish.
M	**Measurable:** A SMART goal is measurable in a readily available and specified way with both interim and summative measures considered.
A	**Attainable:** A SMART goal is challenging, but ultimately achievable. It is a goal for which you and your team are willing to be held accountable.
R	**Relevant:** A SMART goal is tied directly to the specific strengths and challenges associated with your teaching team and with the results you are currently producing with your students. Achieving this goal demands a higher level of effectiveness from everyone.
T	**Time Bound:** A SMART goal can be accomplished in the span of a school year.

Source: Adapted from the work of George T. Doran, 1981.

The key to accomplishing a SMART goal is an action plan. To produce an action plan, the members of an improvement team must think about the steps they will need to move through to accomplish their goal. Without this kind of detail, it is likely that the goal will not be reached. Most action plans include the goal and the final outcome measure that will determine how successful the team has been in pursuing its goal. To make the process manageable, action plans usually include components such as action steps, resources, responsibilities, a timeline, and indicators of success for particular steps in the process. A typical action planning form is displayed in Figure 7.5.

As a team begins to think about moving through this final phase of Focus on the System, team members must consider how they might address their area of challenge. There are at least five different paths a team might take.

1. Use a strategy aligned with your core strength.

    - What are the root causes that enabled the emergence of your core strength?
    - Are there ways in which these areas of strength could be enlisted to address your core challenge?

Figure 7.5 SMART Goals: Action Plan

Smart Goal:	Outcome Measure:

Action Steps to Achieve Smart Goal	Resources Needed	Person(s) Responsible	Timeline	Results (Completion, Quality & Consistency, etc.)

2. Address your area of challenge through its root causes.

   - Begin to address and improve all or most of the root causes associated with your area of challenge.
   - Create specific goals and action plans for each of the root causes.

3. Use value-added information to find other schools with similar demographics that are producing significant growth in your area of challenge.

   - Identify demographically similar schools that are producing large-scale gains in areas where your school is not.
   - Contact the principal of the school.
   - Explore, with representatives of the other school(s), the practices they employ to produce their large-scale gains.

4. Use student projection data to identify the students who have the greatest needs. Note: SAS includes student projection information as part of the EVAAS reporting.

   - Identify the students who are projected to perform poorly in your area of greatest challenge.
   - Provide more time for tasks and additional support in areas where students are especially weak.

5. Devise a creative solution for your area of greatest challenge.

To further clarify the process described in this chapter, an example of a grade-level team's analysis is presented below.

An Example of a Classroom-Level Root Cause Analysis

A fifth-grade team from the HISD examined their achievement and value-added data to identify an area of strength and an area of challenge and then systematically explored what they did that produced these outcomes. Each of the five teachers on the team taught all four core-subject areas—math, reading, science, and social studies—so the grade-level data they examined was a reflection of everyone's teaching. In this particular case, the team members focused most of their attention on the disaggregate-level reporting because this information was most revealing and most interesting.

Figure 7.6 shows the four school diagnostic reports that represent the disaggregated data for this team of teachers. The reports displayed in Figure 7.6 are produced by SAS and are available to districts through the ®Education Value-Added Assessment System (EVAAS) services of SAS Institute, Inc.

Figure 7.6 School Diagnostic Reports: Team of Teachers

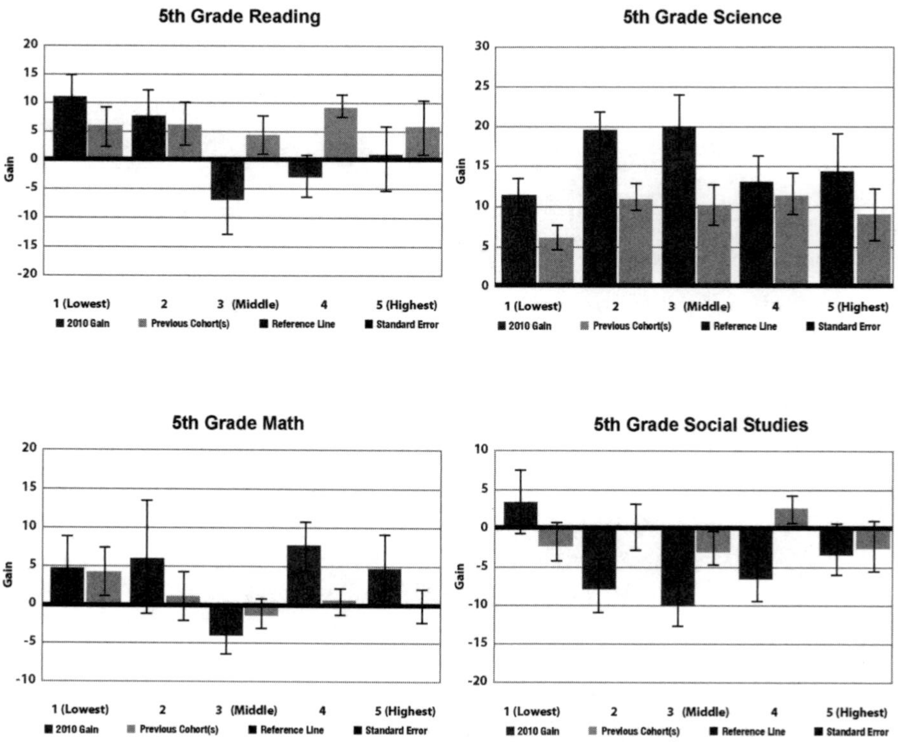
5th Grade Reading
5th Grade Science
5th Grade Math
5th Grade Social Studies
Gain
1 (Lowest)
2
3 (Middle)
4
5 (Highest)
2010 Gain
Previous Cohort(s)
Reference Line
Standard Error

Source: SAS® EVAAS® for K–12 content Copyright ©2011, SAS Institute Inc., Cary, NC, USA, All Rights Reserved. Used with permission.

An interesting pattern was revealed to the team by examining these reports. Science was a clear strength for them. The aggregate-level value-added results in science were very strong, and that strength was also evident in the team's disaggregated science information. With the exception of science, however, these teachers struggled to produce growth with their middle-achieving students (subgroup 3) in each of the disaggregate reports in Figure 7.6. In the science report, all five subgroups experienced more-than-expected growth, and the middle achievers displayed the most growth of the entire group. In the other three subject areas, the growth of middle achievers lagged behind their peers. So for this group of teachers, their area of strength was science instruction, generally, and the growth of middle achievers in science, specifically. The area of challenge for these teachers was the poor growth of middle achieving students in the other three subject areas.

The team then began its strength-based analysis using the strength-based fishbone displayed in Figure 7.7.

In the head of the fishbone the team agreed to write, "High growth in science, especially with middle achieving students." In the course of moving through the factors on the fishbone, the teachers talked about how the curriculum and the instruction they provided in science was different from the curriculum and instruction in the other three subject areas. Under the instructional factors category, the team highlighted *student-friendly learning goals/targets*. Because the big ideas in their science curriculum were broken down into very clear and succinct subcategories, teachers found it easy to create clear, student-friendly learning targets aligned with the state academic content standards.

Under the curriculum and systemic factors category, they highlighted *curricular resources meet student needs*. Here the team was specifically referencing the well-articulated and segmented science curriculum. To make this factor more explicit, the team added *highly segmented curriculum*. This statement really captured the difference between the science curriculum and the other curricula they taught. It was the clarity and the specificity of the segmented science curriculum that allowed teachers to be much more targeted and focused with their instruction in general and especially with their often-overlooked middle achievers.

Under the assessment factors category the team highlighted *regular use of descriptive feedback* and prompted a discussion about how the quality of the curricular resources in science made it much easier to provide really precise feedback to students about where their understandings were relative to where they needed to be. So at the end of their analysis, their fishbone looked like the one in Figure 7.8.

Figure 7.7 Fishbone Diagram: Areas of Strength

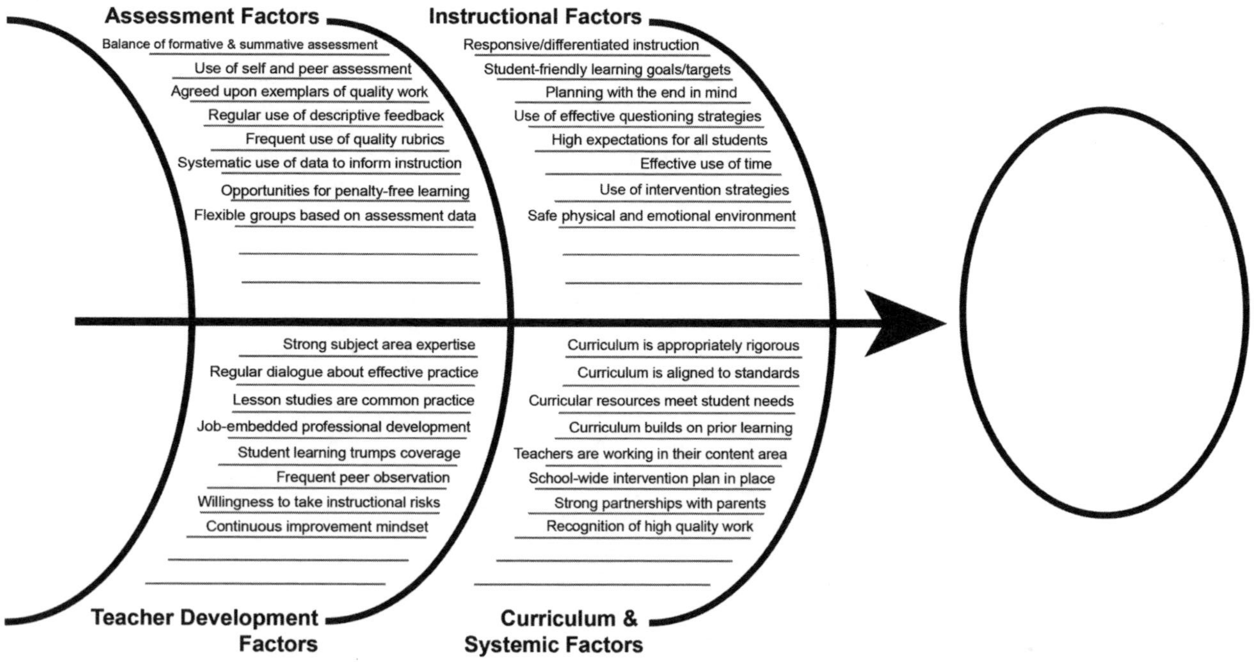

Assessment Factors
Balance of formative & summative assessment
Use of self and peer assessment
Agreed upon exemplars of quality work
Regular use of descriptive feedback
Frequent use of quality rubrics
Systematic use of data to inform instruction
Opportunities for penalty-free learning
Flexible groups based on assessment data
Instructional Factors
Responsive/differentiated instruction
Student-friendly learning goals/targets
Planning with the end in mind
Use of effective questioning strategies
High expectations for all students
Effective use of time
Use of intervention strategies
Safe physical and emotional environment
Strong subject area expertise
Regular dialogue about effective practice
Lesson studies are common practice
Job-embedded professional development
Student learning trumps coverage
Frequent peer observation
Willingness to take instructional risks
Continuous improvement mindset
Teacher Development Factors
Curriculum is appropriately rigorous
Curriculum is aligned to standards
Curricular resources meet student needs
Curriculum builds on prior learning
Teachers are working in their content area
School-wide intervention plan in place
Strong partnerships with parents
Recognition of high quality work
Curriculum & Systemic Factors

Source: © 2011, Battelle for Kids.

Figure 7.8 Completed Fishbone Diagram: Areas of Strength

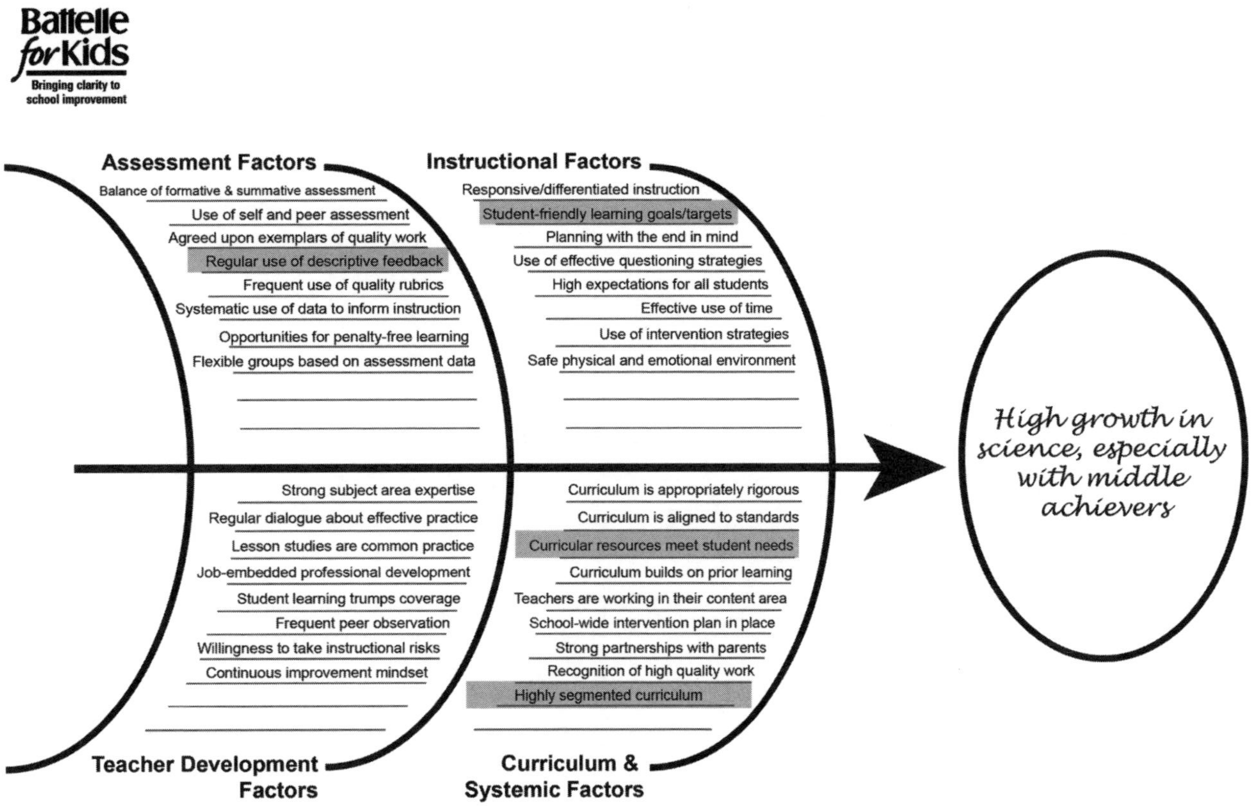
Battelle for Kids
Bringing clarity to school improvement
Assessment Factors
Balance of formative & summative assessment
Use of self and peer assessment
Agreed upon exemplars of quality work
Regular use of descriptive feedback
Frequent use of quality rubrics
Systematic use of data to inform instruction
Opportunities for penalty-free learning
Flexible groups based on assessment data
Instructional Factors
Responsive/differentiated instruction
Student-friendly learning goals/targets
Planning with the end in mind
Use of effective questioning strategies
High expectations for all students
Effective use of time
Use of intervention strategies
Safe physical and emotional environment
Strong subject area expertise
Regular dialogue about effective practice
Lesson studies are common practice
Job-embedded professional development
Student learning trumps coverage
Frequent peer observation
Willingness to take instructional risks
Continuous improvement mindset
Teacher Development Factors
Curriculum is appropriately rigorous
Curriculum is aligned to standards
Curricular resources meet student needs
Curriculum builds on prior learning
Teachers are working in their content area
School-wide intervention plan in place
Strong partnerships with parents
Recognition of high quality work
Highly segmented curriculum
Curriculum & Systemic Factors
High growth in science, especially with middle achievers

Source: © 2011, Battelle for Kids.

As the team moved into its challenge-based analysis they already knew where they wanted to go. They began with the classroom-level challenge-based fishbone illustrated in Figure 7.9.

In many ways, the team's discussion of its area of challenge was a counterpoint to the discussion of its strength. In the head of the fishbone, the team wrote, *poor growth with middle achieving students in math, reading, and social studies*. Under instructional factors, they highlighted *unclear learning goals/targets,* because in comparison to the learning targets for science, the daily targets in the other areas were significantly less specific and clear. Under the curriculum and systemic factors, they highlighted *curriculum resources do not meet students' needs*. These teachers really didn't know that their math, reading, and social studies curricula didn't meet students' needs until they looked at these curricula in comparison to the science curriculum. They also added *poorly segmented curricula* to this category to highlight the difference between the science curriculum materials and the curriculum materials for the other three subject areas. Under the assessment factors, the team highlighted *infrequent use of descriptive feedback*. Again, the quality and usefulness of the feedback given to students is a direct consequence of the clarity and specificity of the learning targets. The result of their analysis is depicted in Figure 7.10.

From this assessment of the team's struggle with middle achieving students in math, reading, and social studies, the team members were ready to design goals for improved practice. Clearly, they needed to work on the curriculum materials associated with their three problem areas. Because social studies was the team's weakest subject area, the five teachers decided to begin their improvement with the learning targets in that subject area.

The team completed its Focus on the System work by creating a SMART goal and an action plan to map out its work over the course of the school year. Their SMART goal was to boost the growth of students in social studies in quintiles 2, 3, and 4 to a level of at least one standard error above expected growth. With their action plan, they decided to use their weekly grade-level meetings to accomplish two things: (1) to develop clearer daily learning targets for students in social studies and (2) to share what had happened as a result of the new learning targets they designed the prior week. At the end of each quarter, the team also decided to compare how its middle achieving students performed on the quarterly assessments in comparison with how middle achieving students had performed on the same assessments the year before.

Figure 7.9 Fishbone Diagram: Areas of Challenge

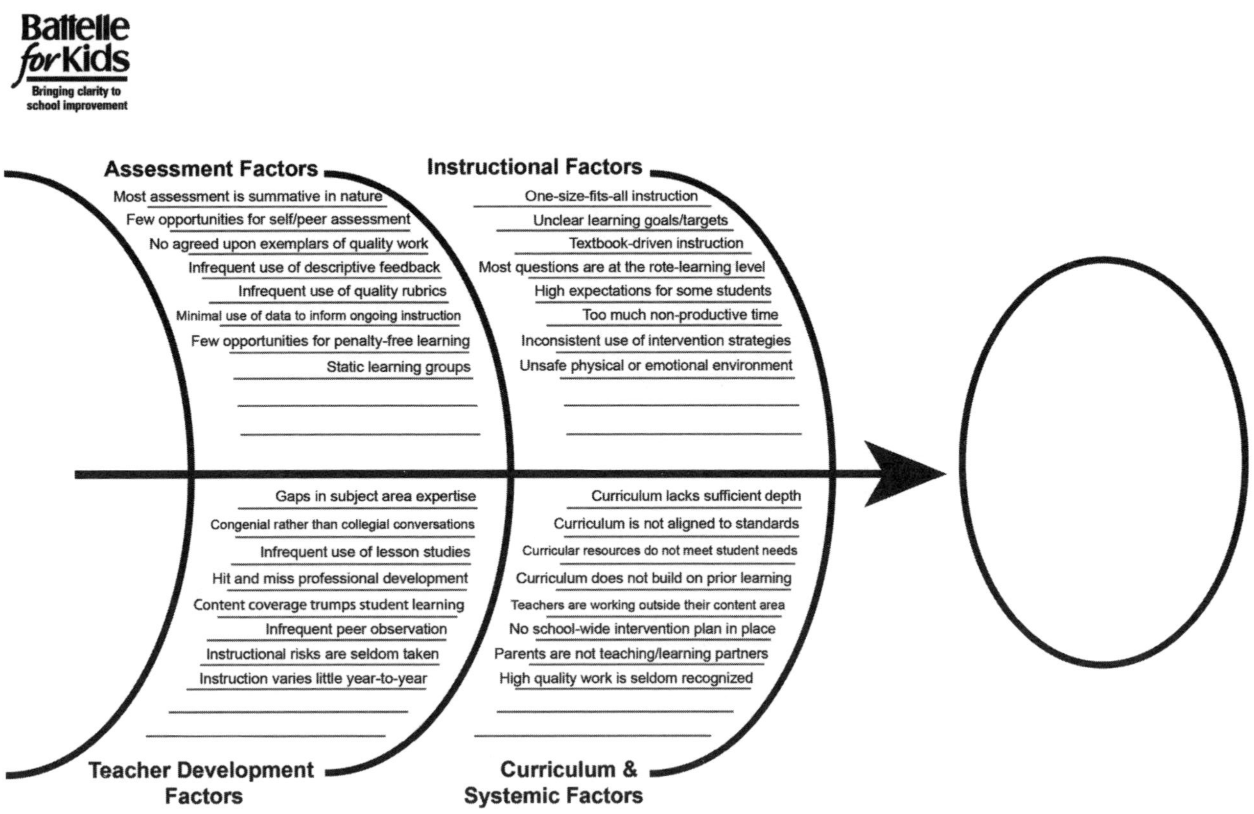

Battelle for Kids
Bringing clarity to school improvement
Assessment Factors
Most assessment is summative in nature
Few opportunities for self/peer assessment
No agreed upon exemplars of quality work
Infrequent use of descriptive feedback
Infrequent use of quality rubrics
Minimal use of data to inform ongoing instruction
Few opportunities for penalty-free learning
Static learning groups
Instructional Factors
One-size-fits-all instruction
Unclear learning goals/targets
Textbook-driven instruction
Most questions are at the rote-learning level
High expectations for some students
Too much non-productive time
Inconsistent use of intervention strategies
Unsafe physical or emotional environment
Gaps in subject area expertise
Congenial rather than collegial conversations
Infrequent use of lesson studies
Hit and miss professional development
Content coverage trumps student learning
Infrequent peer observation
Instructional risks are seldom taken
Instruction varies little year-to-year
Teacher Development Factors
Curriculum lacks sufficient depth
Curriculum is not aligned to standards
Curricular resources do not meet student needs
Curriculum does not build on prior learning
Teachers are working outside their content area
No school-wide intervention plan in place
Parents are not teaching/learning partners
High quality work is seldom recognized
Curriculum & Systemic Factors

Source: © 2011, Battelle for Kids.

Figure 7.10 Completed Fishbone Diagram: Areas of Challenge

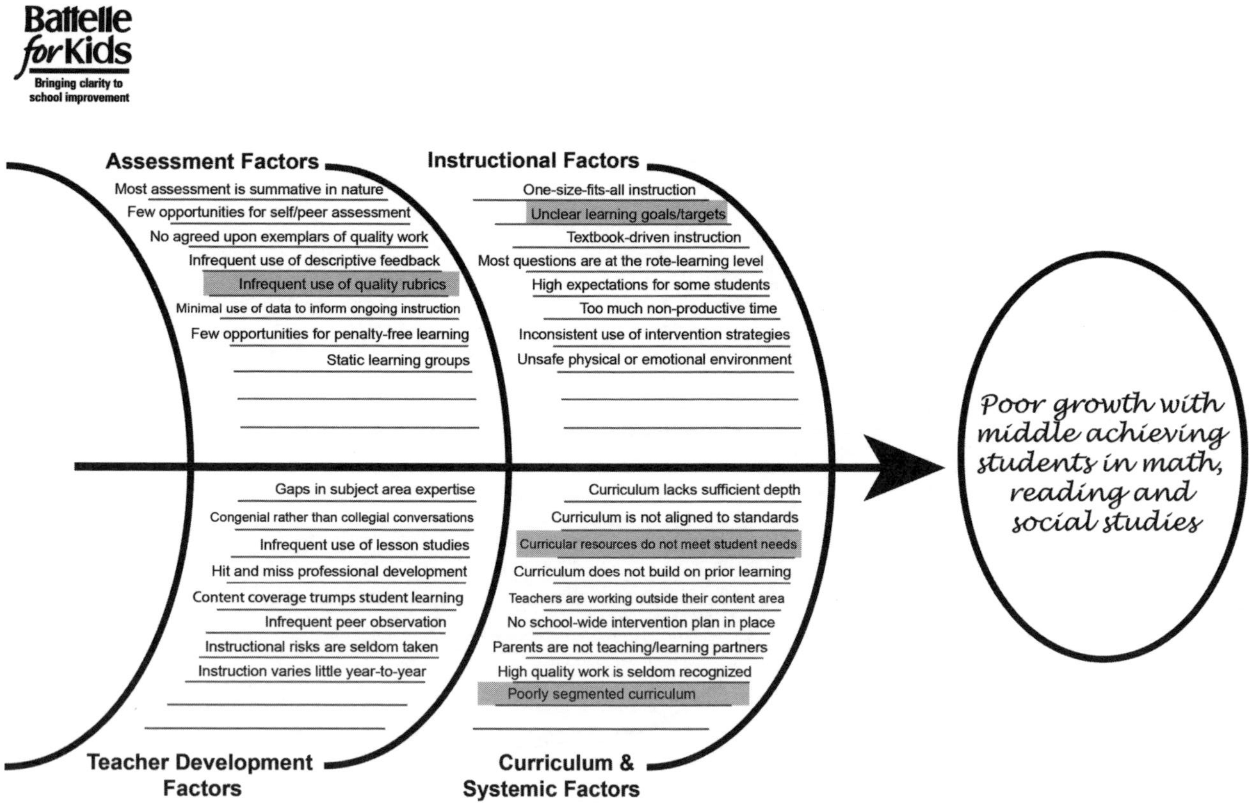

Battelle for Kids
Bringing clarity to school improvement
Assessment Factors
Most assessment is summative in nature
Few opportunities for self/peer assessment
No agreed upon exemplars of quality work
Infrequent use of descriptive feedback
Infrequent use of quality rubrics
Minimal use of data to inform ongoing instruction
Few opportunities for penalty-free learning
Static learning groups
Instructional Factors
One-size-fits-all instruction
Unclear learning goals/targets
Textbook-driven instruction
Most questions are at the rote-learning level
High expectations for some students
Too much non-productive time
Inconsistent use of intervention strategies
Unsafe physical or emotional environment
Gaps in subject area expertise
Congenial rather than collegial conversations
Infrequent use of lesson studies
Hit and miss professional development
Content coverage trumps student learning
Infrequent peer observation
Instructional risks are seldom taken
Instruction varies little year-to-year
Teacher Development Factors
Curriculum lacks sufficient depth
Curriculum is not aligned to standards
Curricular resources do not meet student needs
Curriculum does not build on prior learning
Teachers are working outside their content area
No school-wide intervention plan in place
Parents are not teaching/learning partners
High quality work is seldom recognized
Poorly segmented curriculum
Curriculum & Systemic Factors
Poor growth with middle achieving students in math, reading and social studies

Source: © 2011, Battelle for Kids.

Exploring Root Causes at the School and District Levels

Root cause analysis looks very much the same at the school and district levels. The only differences are (1) the work emerges out of higher level data and (2) the fishbones look a little different to account for the different kinds of work in which school and district leaders engage. In both cases, however, the key to the work lies in helping participants accept responsibility for the results their school or district produces.

Working With Higher Level Data

At the district level, a leadership team should focus most of its attention on large-scale patterns that reflect the quality of learning across a large segment of the district population. Similarly, at the school level, a school-based team should focus on large-scale patterns that reflect the quality of learning across a large segment of the school population. By focusing attention on large-scale patterns, these teams have an opportunity to make a real difference across large segments of the student population.

School- and District-Level Fishbones

Samples of strength- and challenge-based fishbones designed specifically for the school and district level are included in the hands-on resource guide at the end of this chapter. Although these fishbones are similar to the classroom-level fishbones, they differ slightly because of the kinds of work in which leaders at these levels engage. It is worth repeating that to make this process work at these levels of an organization, school and district leaders must be willing to take responsibility for the current state of their system. In many cases, challenges arise because leaders have not put in place the appropriate structures to promote the right kinds of collegial conversations. A particular high-level challenge may also arise because the appropriate leadership may not have been exercised to deal with a problem before it became a large-scale problem. Whatever the case, the act of taking responsibility is a necessary first step toward addressing the challenge.

> School and district leaders must be willing to take responsibility for the current state of their system.

Once building and district-level teams identify the root causes of their most significant strengths and challenges, they should produce a SMART goal and action plan for addressing their core challenge. Whenever possible, these same teams should work to leverage their strengths in ways to address their challenges.

Summary

The primary purpose of this chapter is to introduce the concept of root cause analysis. By understanding why things occur as they do, we have the opportunity to leverage organizational strengths and address organizational challenges. The first step in either of these activities is to accept responsibility for the outcomes the organization generates. With the acceptance of responsibility, we have the means for improvement. In Chapter 8 we share some stories of district-, building-, and classroom-level teams that have used their value-added and achievement results to leverage improvement across their organization.

Action Steps and Reflection Questions

Action Step: Put together a team to collaboratively conduct root cause analysis.

- Who might facilitate the team to make sure the process flows?
- Who will you include on the team? Consider teachers, leadership, and support personnel.
- How much time will you set aside to go through this process?

Action Step: Begin root cause analysis by considering areas of strength.

- What factors (see hands-on resource guide) might have contributed to your area of strength?
- What factors actually led to getting your good results?

Action Step: Continue the root cause analysis by considering areas of challenge.

- What factors (see hands-on resource guide) might have contributed to your area of challenge?
- What factors actually led to getting your substandard results?

Action Step: Produce a SMART goal and an action plan.

- Have you limited yourself to a reasonable number of goals? Consider creating only one or two goals, so that you can focus on making your goals a reality.

- Are your goals strategic, measurable, attainable, relevant, and able to be accomplished within a school year?
- How might your action plan help you realize your SMART goal? Consider action steps you'll need to take, resources you might need, who will be involved, and the timeline.

Hands-on Resource Guide for Teachers and Leaders

- System-Level Fishbones (see Figures 7.11 and 7.12)
- Building-Level Fishbones (see Figures 7.13 and 7.14)
- SMART Goals: Action Plan (see Figure 7.15)

Figure 7.11 System-Level Strength Fishbone

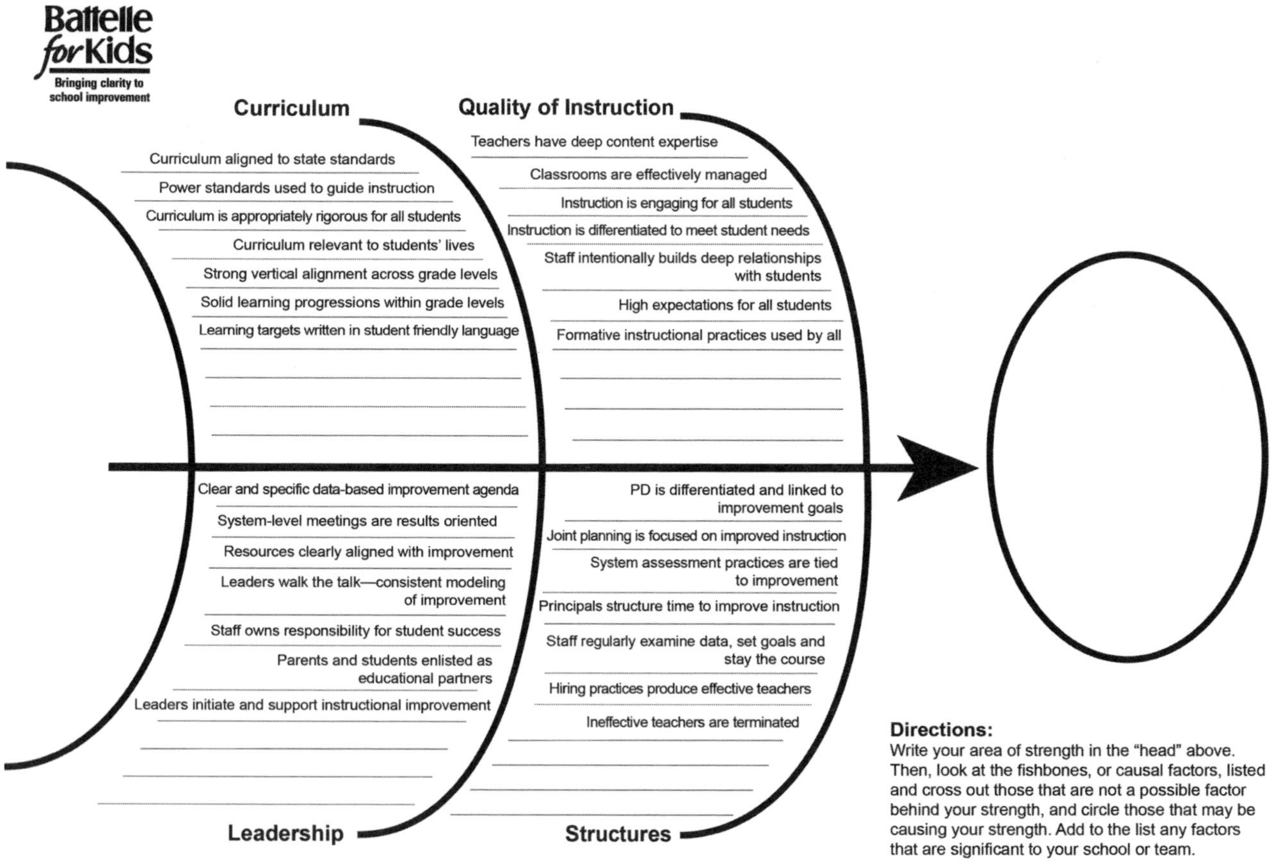
Battelle for Kids
Bringing clarity to school improvement
Curriculum
Curriculum aligned to state standards
Power standards used to guide instruction
Curriculum is appropriately rigorous for all students
Curriculum relevant to students' lives
Strong vertical alignment across grade levels
Solid learning progressions within grade levels
Learning targets written in student friendly language
Quality of Instruction
Teachers have deep content expertise
Classrooms are effectively managed
Instruction is engaging for all students
Instruction is differentiated to meet student needs
Staff intentionally builds deep relationships with students
High expectations for all students
Formative instructional practices used by all
Clear and specific data-based improvement agenda
System-level meetings are results oriented
Resources clearly aligned with improvement
Leaders walk the talk—consistent modeling of improvement
Staff owns responsibility for student success
Parents and students enlisted as educational partners
Leaders initiate and support instructional improvement
Leadership
PD is differentiated and linked to improvement goals
Joint planning is focused on improved instruction
System assessment practices are tied to improvement
Principals structure time to improve instruction
Staff regularly examine data, set goals and stay the course
Hiring practices produce effective teachers
Ineffective teachers are terminated
Structures
Directions:
Write your area of strength in the "head" above. Then, look at the fishbones, or causal factors, listed and cross out those that are not a possible factor behind your strength, and circle those that may be causing your strength. Add to the list any factors that are significant to your school or team.

Source: © 2011, Battelle for Kids.

Figure 7.12 System-Level Challenge Fishbone

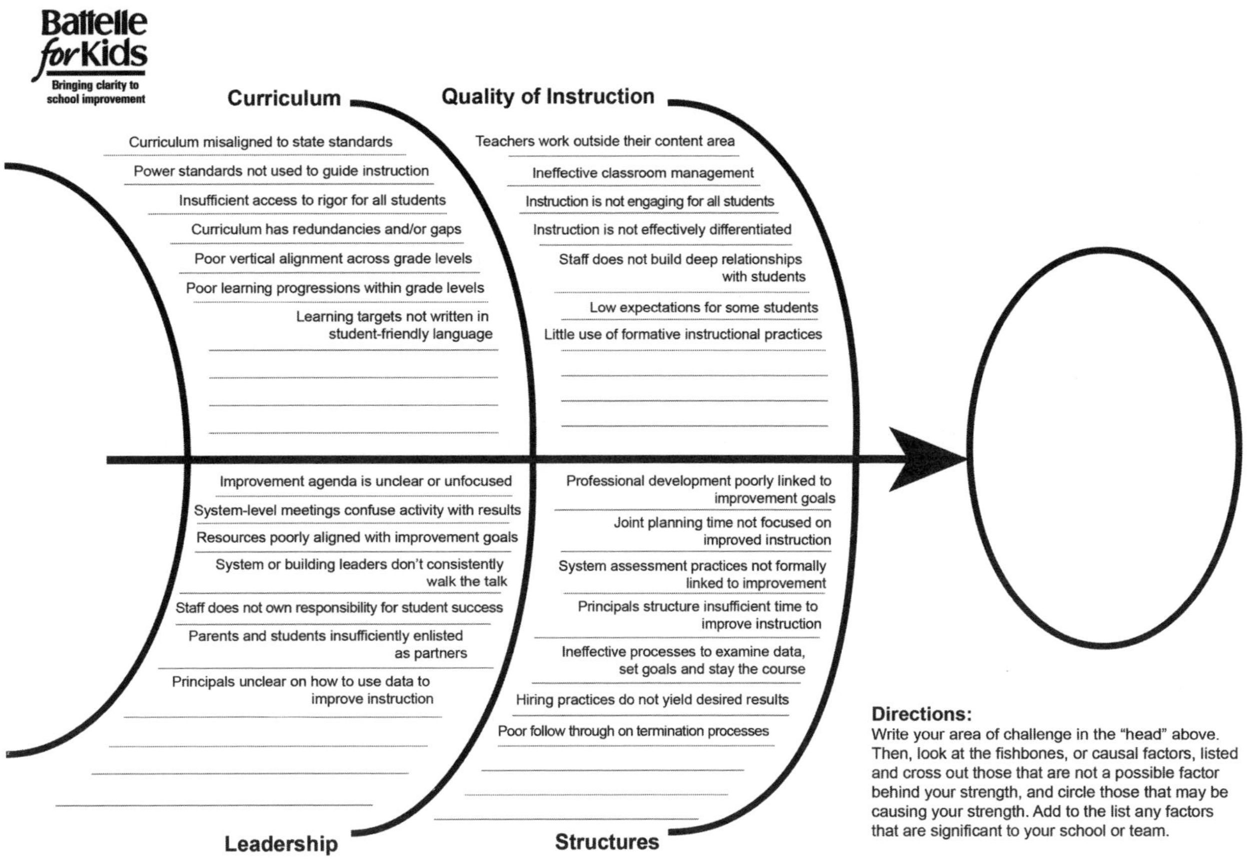
Battelle for Kids
Bringing clarity to school improvement
Curriculum
Curriculum misaligned to state standards
Power standards not used to guide instruction
Insufficient access to rigor for all students
Curriculum has redundancies and/or gaps
Poor vertical alignment across grade levels
Poor learning progressions within grade levels
Learning targets not written in student-friendly language
Quality of Instruction
Teachers work outside their content area
Ineffective classroom management
Instruction is not engaging for all students
Instruction is not effectively differentiated
Staff does not build deep relationships with students
Low expectations for some students
Little use of formative instructional practices
Improvement agenda is unclear or unfocused
System-level meetings confuse activity with results
Resources poorly aligned with improvement goals
System or building leaders don't consistently walk the talk
Staff does not own responsibility for student success
Parents and students insufficiently enlisted as partners
Principals unclear on how to use data to improve instruction
Leadership
Professional development poorly linked to improvement goals
Joint planning time not focused on improved instruction
System assessment practices not formally linked to improvement
Principals structure insufficient time to improve instruction
Ineffective processes to examine data, set goals and stay the course
Hiring practices do not yield desired results
Poor follow through on termination processes
Structures
Directions:
Write your area of challenge in the "head" above. Then, look at the fishbones, or causal factors, listed and cross out those that are not a possible factor behind your strength, and circle those that may be causing your strength. Add to the list any factors that are significant to your school or team.

Source: © 2011, Battelle for Kids.

Figure 7.13 Building-Level Strength Fishbone

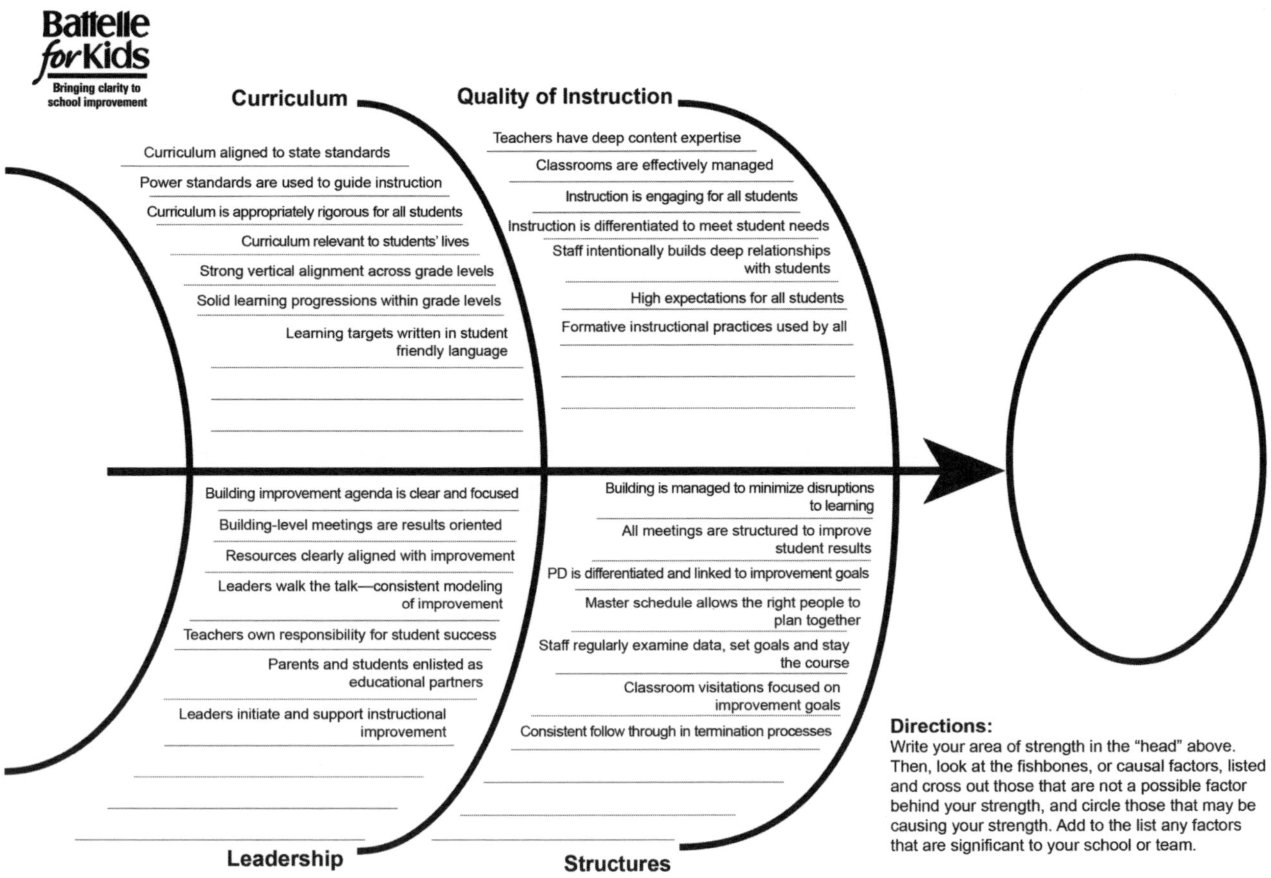
Battelle for Kids
Bringing clarity to school improvement
Curriculum
Curriculum aligned to state standards
Power standards are used to guide instruction
Curriculum is appropriately rigorous for all students
Curriculum relevant to students' lives
Strong vertical alignment across grade levels
Solid learning progressions within grade levels
Learning targets written in student friendly language
Quality of Instruction
Teachers have deep content expertise
Classrooms are effectively managed
Instruction is engaging for all students
Instruction is differentiated to meet student needs
Staff intentionally builds deep relationships with students
High expectations for all students
Formative instructional practices used by all
Leadership
Building improvement agenda is clear and focused
Building-level meetings are results oriented
Resources clearly aligned with improvement
Leaders walk the talk—consistent modeling of improvement
Teachers own responsibility for student success
Parents and students enlisted as educational partners
Leaders initiate and support instructional improvement
Structures
Building is managed to minimize disruptions to learning
All meetings are structured to improve student results
PD is differentiated and linked to improvement goals
Master schedule allows the right people to plan together
Staff regularly examine data, set goals and stay the course
Classroom visitations focused on improvement goals
Consistent follow through in termination processes
Directions:
Write your area of strength in the "head" above. Then, look at the fishbones, or causal factors, listed and cross out those that are not a possible factor behind your strength, and circle those that may be causing your strength. Add to the list any factors that are significant to your school or team.

Source: © 2011, Battelle for Kids.

Figure 7.14 Building-Level Challenge Fishbone

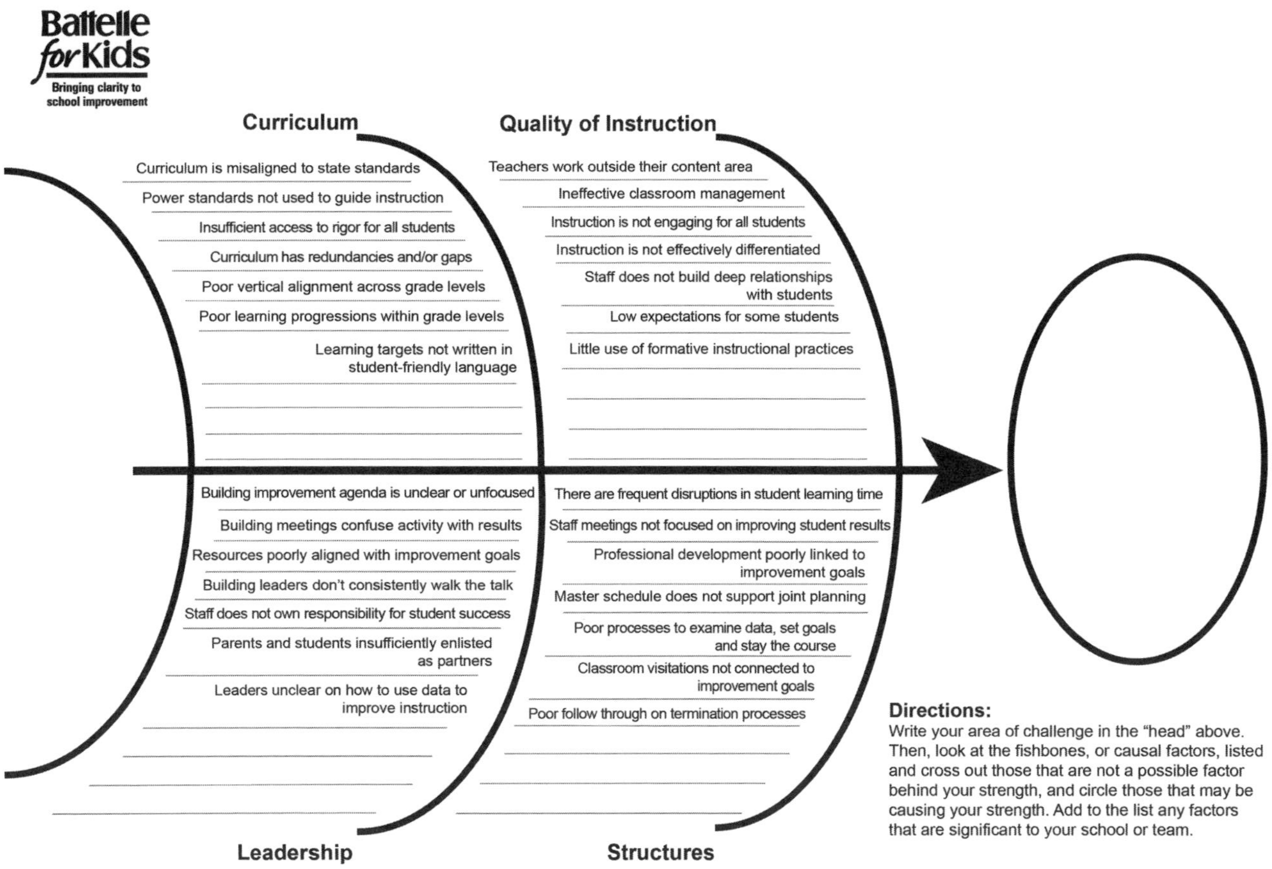

Battelle for Kids
Bringing clarity to school improvement
Curriculum
Curriculum is misaligned to state standards
Power standards not used to guide instruction
Insufficient access to rigor for all students
Curriculum has redundancies and/or gaps
Poor vertical alignment across grade levels
Poor learning progressions within grade levels
Learning targets not written in student-friendly language
Quality of Instruction
Teachers work outside their content area
Ineffective classroom management
Instruction is not engaging for all students
Instruction is not effectively differentiated
Staff does not build deep relationships with students
Low expectations for some students
Little use of formative instructional practices
Leadership
Building improvement agenda is unclear or unfocused
Building meetings confuse activity with results
Resources poorly aligned with improvement goals
Building leaders don't consistently walk the talk
Staff does not own responsibility for student success
Parents and students insufficiently enlisted as partners
Leaders unclear on how to use data to improve instruction
Structures
There are frequent disruptions in student learning time
Staff meetings not focused on improving student results
Professional development poorly linked to improvement goals
Master schedule does not support joint planning
Poor processes to examine data, set goals and stay the course
Classroom visitations not connected to improvement goals
Poor follow through on termination processes
Directions:
Write your area of challenge in the "head" above. Then, look at the fishbones, or causal factors, listed and cross out those that are not a possible factor behind your strength, and circle those that may be causing your strength. Add to the list any factors that are significant to your school or team.

Source: © 2011, Battelle for Kids.

Figure 7.15 SMART Goals: Outcome Measure Example

Smart Goal:	Outcome Measure:

Action Steps to Achieve Smart Goal	Resources Needed	Person(s) Responsible	Timeline	Results (Completion, Quality & Consistency, etc.)

Source: © 2011, Battelle for Kids.

8

Step V

Take Action, Monitor, and Adjust

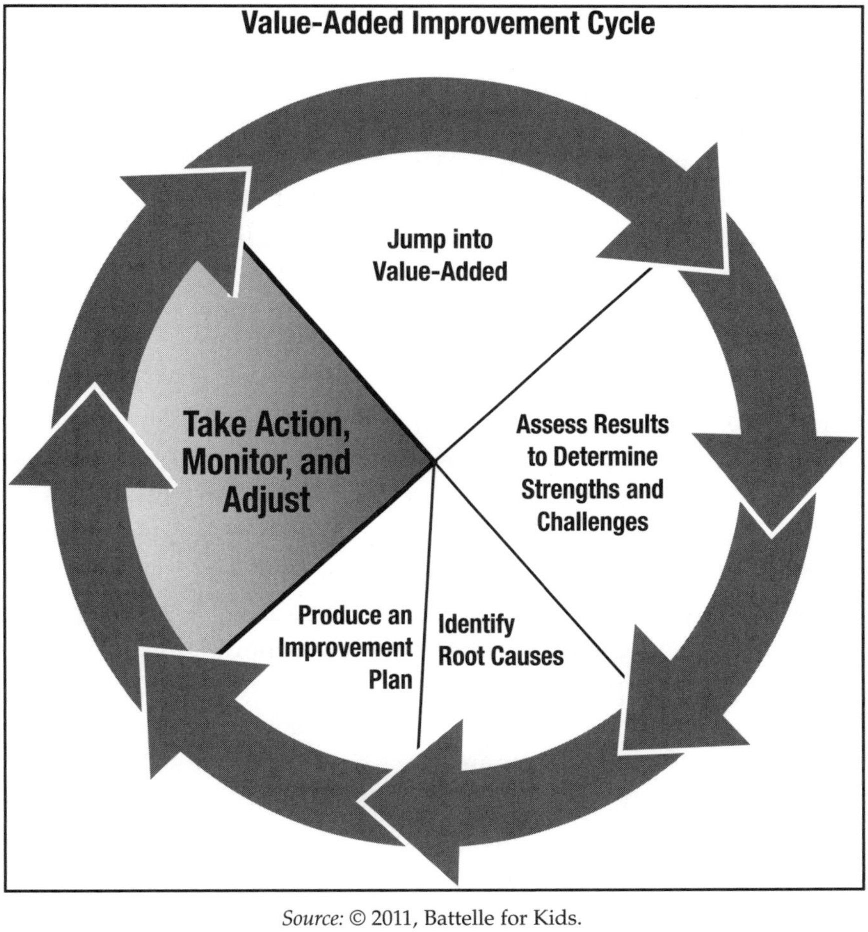
Value-Added Improvement Cycle
Jump into Value-Added
Assess Results to Determine Strengths and Challenges
Identify Root Causes
Produce an Improvement Plan
Take Action, Monitor, and Adjust

Source: © 2011, Battelle for Kids.

Chapter 8 Core Concepts

1. Act on value-added information by implementing your improvement plan.
2. Monitor implementation of your plan and adjust your actions as needed.
3. Evaluate the success of your improvement plan.
4. Equip educators to collaboratively explore value-added information.
5. Begin anew with fresh data.

Overview: Take Action, Monitor, and Adjust

When Bobby Moore began his new job as the principal of Canaan Middle School in rural Ohio, he really didn't know what to expect. He was charged with reconfiguring a school where most kids were passing the state tests, where staff members were collegial with one another, and where teachers did an excellent job of building relationships with students. But when Bobby saw his school's value-added reports, he knew something was wrong: Almost all of the reports were dominated by the color red. His staff was producing less-than-expected gains with students in almost all core subject areas. The lone exception—the one area where teachers were producing expected gains—was sixth-grade math. Bobby knew that he and his staff had a lot of work to do.

As he began his first year, Bobby wanted to make sure that his staff understood the information that was contained in his school's value-added and achievement reports, but he also wanted to make sure that his staff didn't spend all of their time just talking about the problems. He was interested in helping his staff commit to taking the kinds of action that would lead to improvement. To make this happen, Bobby spent time with his staff examining both their value-added and achievement information at the school level, at the level of teacher teams, and in a variety of one-on-one meetings. During those early days, they made use of many of the ideas described in Chapters 3 through 6. Fortunately, for his teachers and his students, that is not where they stopped. Instead of simply identifying their problems, as happens in some schools, Bobby's staff looked for root causes and, ultimately, for solutions. The next two years were hard work, but teachers continued to plan, take action, assess their results, and adjust. Over the course of two years, they saw the information in their value-added reports go from almost all red to almost all green.

Chapter 8 builds on the work of the first seven chapters by discussing one of the most important but often missing aspects of the entire process: taking action, monitoring results, adjusting plans and strategies as necessary, and evaluating the success of the whole process.

Concept 1: Act on Value-Added Information by Implementing Your Improvement Plan

Bobby Moore loves to use movies to illustrate important points. In one conversation with him, he compared normal schooling to the movie *Rambo: First Blood, Part II*. Bobby focused on Rambo's mission: Rambo was sent to Vietnam, not to rescue MIAs but simply to document that many of them were still being held prisoner. "That's what schools do all the time," explained Bobby. "We have our kids, who are prisoners in schools. We take snapshots all the time of kids struggling, not learning, and not growing, but we don't adapt (our instructional strategies) and rescue them. We collect data and take snapshots, but we leave them there." So from Bobby's perspective, the missing piece in school reform is action.

One of the changes Bobby and his staff made in their school was in response to some of their disaggregated value-added data. When they examined their Adequate Yearly Progress (AYP) subgroup data, they discovered that students with disabilities were making good gains in science and social studies but less than expected gains in math and reading. What was the difference? Students with disabilities received math and reading instruction in a self-contained resource room in the basement of the school; in social studies and science, these same students were included in the regular fifth- and sixth-grade classrooms. The first step, then, was to create more inclusive opportunities for students who receive special education services. Replicating successful practices—and ditching those that aren't—is one important way that educators use value-added information to improve practice.

Bobby's staff also decided to alter the master schedule. They shaved four minutes off of each period in their day to create a new instructional period. This change added five periods of intervention per week to allow teachers to respond to the data and give students additional support as needed. They nicknamed these periods *No New*

Instruction (NNI). These intervention periods were constructed to be flexible. Teachers worked together to determine which students would receive intervention in which areas, and they changed the intervention rosters often. As a part of this strategy, the staff also developed their own program of tiered interventions. As a result of this intervention model, they no longer find it necessary to do after-school tutoring.

Concept 2: Monitor Implementation of Your Plan and Adjust Your Actions as Needed

After putting these changes in place, Bobby and his staff were pleased to see a higher level of engagement from their students with disabilities, so they had at least some validation that a part of their plan worked. But they also monitored other aspects of their plan, using formative assessment strategies to determine if students mastered each day's, or each week's, learning targets. For those students who were able to demonstrate that they had mastered the material, their NNI period became an enrichment period.

In the few cases where the first level of intervention didn't work—targeted intervention in the extra NNI period—teachers were charged with inventing different, more intensive interventions. These included small group work, and in some cases, more practice at home. If those interventions didn't produce acceptable results, then the next level included help from the special education director and the school psychologist. Teachers worked with these professionals to brainstorm additional strategies to help students reach mastery. As teachers continued to develop this program, they met every three weeks to go over student data and discuss additional intervention strategies.

Two Kinds of Monitoring

The Canaan story exemplifies how a leader and his staff can improve the results they are getting with their students. A big part of this process is monitoring. Monitoring, as it is being used here, really takes two forms: monitoring processes and monitoring outcomes.

Process monitoring is conducted to answer the question, *Are we doing what we said we would do*? The purpose of this kind of monitoring is to hold team members accountable for what they said they were going to do. As a general rule it is important to do this kind of work with a team rather than to a team. One of the best ways to achieve this is to be clear about planning processes, the outcomes of planning processes, and the support that will be provided for change. When teachers know what they are supposed to accomplish in meetings and that someone is paying attention to the results of their work, the team is much more likely to hold itself accountable. Teacher teams also conduct process monitoring by actually spending time in each other's classrooms. The primary purpose of these visits is to provide additional support to team members as they begin to experiment with new strategies.

School leaders and coaches may also participate in process monitoring by conducting observations or walk-throughs that are specifically designed to give teachers descriptive feedback relative to the implementation of their plan. The walk-through technique is based on the work of Carolyn Downey and her colleagues (Downey, Steffy, English, Frase, & Poston, 2004). Walk-throughs are intended to be separate from formal teacher evaluation processes. Their primary purpose is to promote dialogue and reflection about teaching practices and school-related goals.

Besides monitoring processes, teams must also monitor results. In the first chapter we briefly described the importance of a balanced assessment system that employs both formative and summative measures in an iterative cycle. In this model, the process of instruction continuously produces artifacts that are assessed for the purposes of improving instruction. We think it is appropriate to return to the Balanced Assessment Cycle (see Figure 8.1) because it is a perfect example of how both short- and long-term results monitoring is connected to instructional improvement.

This model is grounded in years of research on formative instructional practices (Hattie, 2009). An in-depth discussion of these practices is beyond the scope of this book, but we recommend that school leaders and teachers become knowledgeable about the tenets of sound formative instruction practices because they illustrate conclusively the relationship between monitoring and improvement.

The Canaan Middle School staff uses four different lenses to monitor instructional outcomes: common classroom assessment data; state achievement test information; value-added information; and parent, teacher, community, and student survey data. The use of multiple lenses to monitor and adjust their curriculum and instruction is a key aspect of their success. The use of multiple lenses is so ingrained in this staff that even when they receive information that students performed well on state achievement tests, they downplay

Figure 8.1 A Balanced Assessment Cycle

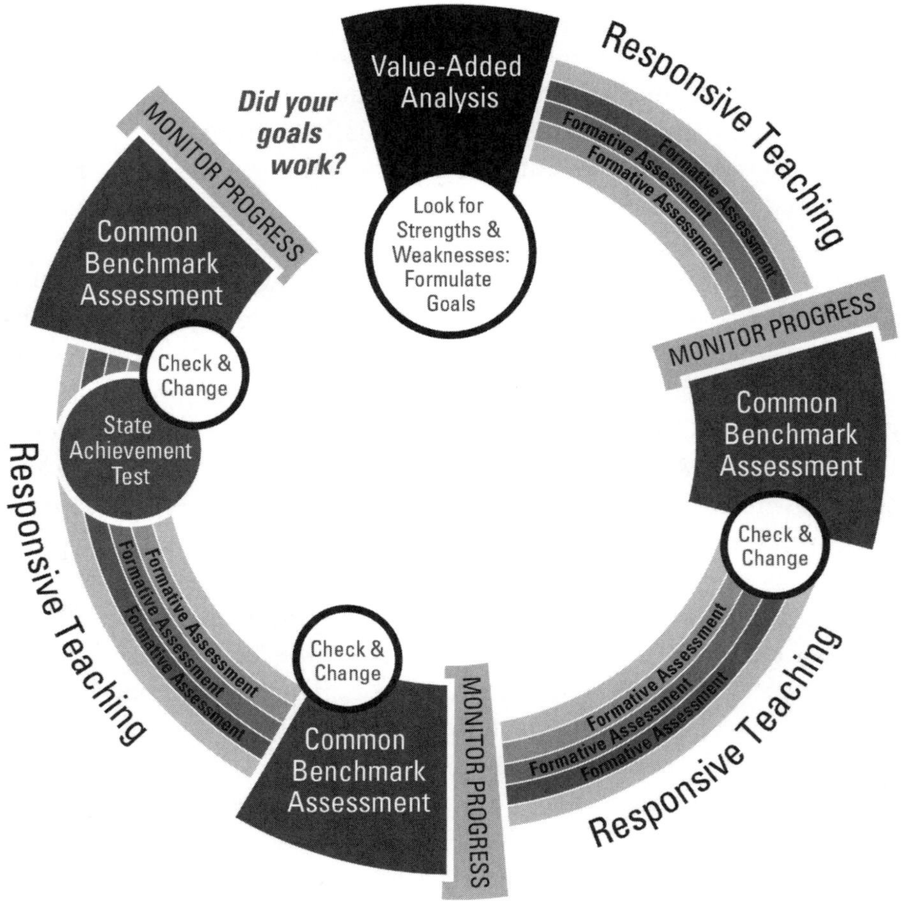

Value-Added Analysis
Look for Strengths & Weaknesses: Formulate Goals
Did your goals work?
MONITOR PROGRESS
Common Benchmark Assessment
Check & Change
State Achievement Test
Responsive Teaching
Formative Assessment
Formative Assessment
Formative Assessment
MONITOR PROGRESS
Common Benchmark Assessment
Check & Change
Responsive Teaching
Formative Assessment
Formative Assessment
Formative Assessment
MONITOR PROGRESS
Common Benchmark Assessment
Check & Change
Responsive Teaching
Formative Assessment
Formative Assessment
Formative Assessment

Source: © 2011, Battelle for Kids.

its importance until they get verification through their value-added reports. Once they receive this level of confirmation, they then evaluate their successes and plan for other improvements.

Concept 3: Evaluate the Success of Your Improvement Plan

Katie Hartley, a fifth-grade math teacher in an elementary school in rural Ohio, wasn't satisfied when she looked at her first round of value-added reports. She saw that she was producing expected levels of growth in the aggregate, but when she examined her subgroup data she discovered that she was producing much more growth with her high achievers than her low achievers. In fact, her low achievers were not making expected gains. As Katie thought about her value-added results, she began to think in terms of root causes. She concluded there were gaps in her school's math curriculum relative to the state's fifth-grade math standards. She also believed that she could be doing more on a daily basis to improve the growth of her lower achievers. She decided to make some changes.

Changes included designing supplemental materials to augment her current math program as well as creating additional math units to fill in the gaps that characterized the current program. Determined to increase her student's growth, Katie also improved how she used in-class assessments, creating both summative and formative assessments aligned to state academic content standards. She used the formative assessments to make sure her students were mastering the daily and weekly material and to adjust her teaching as needed.

The results from these modifications were encouraging. Her value-added results at the end of the year looked markedly different. Now, all of her students were experiencing more-than-expected growth, but interestingly, she saw essentially the same pattern in her data: Her higher achieving students were still making larger gains than her lower achieving students (see Chapter 6 for discussion on how to find similar trends in your value-added data). She decided that she wasn't providing enough review for students who hadn't mastered the material the first time around. If these students don't get additional intervention or more time to practice, they are often left even further behind.

As a result of this analysis, Katie decided to implement additional changes in the new school year. She created weekly review sheets, consisting of twenty problems addressing twenty different skills. Students were also required to rework assignments until they reached mastery. Another strategy Katie employed was to ask high school juniors and seniors to come during study hall periods to tutor individual fifth-grade students on the math skills they hadn't yet mastered. Katie also instituted a math facts program to ensure that students were mastering basic math facts. This helped students to be more efficient as they solved math problems.

At the end of the second year, Katie anxiously awaited her value-added reports to evaluate whether these changes had made a difference. They had. The reports showed, once again, students were growing far more than expected. Her low-achieving students were now making very strong gains. Interestingly, all of the changes she had introduced to provide better support for her low achievers also seemed to be benefitting her high achievers. Her middle and high achievers continued to make more growth than her low achievers. This is a phenomenon we often see when teachers get serious about improving their instruction. The changes they make to produce greater achievement gains with one group of students often benefit that group and other students as well.

In the case of Katie Hartley, each year's value-added information was cause for celebration, affirmation, and validation, but each year's data also provided reasons to make even more improvements. Value-added reports are important instructional mirrors. They provide teachers the opportunity to take an objective look at their practice and to explore the efficacy of different instruction and assessment practices. Katie improved, but her students were the real winners.

Concept 4: Begin Anew With Fresh Data

For Katie, each new school year meant new students and new value-added reports. The beginning of each year became an opportunity not only to reflect but also to start anew. The ritual of examining her value-added data school year has become as important a tradition as creating fresh bulletin boards.

Heather Dzikiy, who we met in Chapter 2, is also a veteran of using the value-added improvement cycle. Heather teaches fourth grade in rural Pennsylvania.

The first time Heather looked at her value-added data she was dismayed to discover that she was apparently teaching to the middle. She said that when she saw her teacher-level value-added report, which uses students' prior proficiency levels to disaggregate her classroom into low-, middle-, and high-achieving subgroups (see sample report in Chapter 6), what she saw was "alarming." This report confirmed that her middle and lower achieving students were progressing at expected rates but her highest achieving students weren't growing nearly as much. As Heather told us, "I was leaving out the top-end kids, which surprised me, because I thought if anybody, they would be getting what they needed. They were growing but not at the rate that they could. That's where I was really concerned."

In conversations with Heather, she described some of the specific changes she made as a result of analyzing her value-added reports. She began using a more individualized phonics approach, employing the Words Their Way program. While visiting, we observed this new approach in action. During phonics time, three leveled groups of students were working on word patterns that had been specially selected according to areas of weakness from the previous week of instruction. Heather made these changes specifically because she felt her data revealed that she was teaching mostly to the middle, and she wanted to make sure her instruction was also impacting low-achieving as well as high-achieving students.

In addition, Heather began organizing reading instruction around literature circles, using the Dynamic Indicators of Basic Early Literacy Skills (DIBELS) assessment data and informal classroom assessment data to make decisions about how kids would be grouped. Her new literature circles were "based on the data, instead of just the kids' interest or my choosing." During literature circle time, we saw kids reading independently and in small groups around the room, confidently marking which reading strategies they were using. Heather worked with small groups during this time; for some groups she chose an extension; with others, an intervention activity.

In a conversation with Heather and her principal, Elizabeth Shindledecker, they talked about how they had been using a reading comprehension program that wasn't working, a fact they realized after analyzing their achievement and value-added results in reading. Both the achievement and value-added results were low. Said Heather, "We've gotten away from giving book review tests and some of the other stodgy, traditional methods that weren't telling us what we needed to know." They decided to bring in a consultant to guide them in a new direction, and they are now using a different approach to teach reading that focuses on high-impact reading strategies.

Now that they've started using new reading and spelling curricula, not only are students performing better on the state achievement test, but they're also more engaged and more involved in their own learning. As Heather told us, "Value-added information gives me an excuse to change and allows me to track my changes, like a map."

Heather's teacher-level value-added reports inspired her to differentiate her instruction to meet the varied needs of her students. These changes paid off. As Heather notes, "My high kids caught up to where I wanted them to be. All kids—low, middle, and high—were growing." But these weren't the only changes Heather made in response to her data. As she began to look at the value-added reports from her other subject areas, she could see that her highest gains were in reading. While her math results were satisfactory, she wondered if she couldn't boost her math gains by trying some new things in math, as well.

Heather demonstrated data-driven decisions in action. She responded to her data initially by changing how she taught reading. Later, she also changed her approach to teaching mathematics. Heather's advice to fellow teachers: "Don't be afraid to make changes in what you're doing. Most changes have a positive outcome. Being flexible and willing to try something new or different can make a really big difference."

Summary

The success of teachers and leaders like Bobby, Heather, and Katie is not accidental. What transformed the schools and the classrooms we've described throughout this book is straightforward: thoughtful, deliberate implementation of the five-step value-added improvement cycle. Although none of our partners use the cycle in exactly the same way, what they all have in common is that they begin by jumping into value-added analysis. Second, they spend time interpreting their results and determining their strengths and challenges. Third, they work collaboratively to identify the root causes of their most significant strengths and challenges. Fourth, they use this information to develop an improvement plan. Finally, they act on that plan, monitor their results, and adjust their practice as necessary. And they don't stop there. They continue the next year by using new value-added and achievement information to further evaluate the efficacy of their program and to begin the cycle of inquiry and improvement again. All of the educators identified in our success stories share a relentless need to improve student learning, the heart to mercilessly dig into their own practices, and the courage to try new strategies and reject those that aren't working. We feel confident that you, too, can use this cycle to produce your own success stories, whether you're a teacher, a leader, or in a support role.

Action Steps and Reflection Questions

Action Step: Discuss your improvement plan with your colleagues, and brainstorm specific actions that you will take to make the plan a reality.

- What will it take to make your improvement plan a reality?
- What concerns you the most about your improvement plan? What ideas do you have for tackling anticipated challenges?
- What resources do you need to ensure your plan is successful?

Action Step: Monitor the implementation of your improvement plan throughout the school year.

- Who will be responsible for monitoring the implementation of your plan?
- What will you do to monitor implementation throughout the school year?
- How will you build collaborative inquiry and shared responsibility for monitoring the success of your improvement plan?

Hands-On Resource Guide for Teachers and Leaders

- Reflection and Discussion Protocol for Professional Learning Teams (see Figure 8.2)
- Self-Evaluation for School Leaders (see Figure 8.3)

Figure 8.2 Reflection and Discussion Protocol for Professional Learning Teams

In your professional learning team, discuss the following questions.

1. What are the specific actions that you plan on taking as a result of conducting a root cause analysis and creating an improvement plan? List your top three actions below.

   a.

   b.

   c.

2. What resources do you need to make these actions a reality? Discuss with your team and record your thoughts.

3. How do you plan on monitoring whether your plan is working or not? Consider formative assessment data as well as summative data, including next year's value-added reports.

Figure 8.3 Self-Evaluation for School Leaders

The purpose of this self-evaluation is to help school leaders think about where they are in terms of acting on their improvement plans.

Directions: Using the 1–5 agreeability scale, evaluate your leadership practices for each of the statements in the chart below.

1 = Strongly disagree

2 = Disagree

3 = Neutral or unsure

4 = Agree

5 = Strongly agree

Reflection Statement	*Self-Rating*
1. I feel prepared to implement our improvement plan. I know where I will start and how I will proceed.	
2. I have, or know how to get, the resources I need to act on our improvement plan.	
3. I feel confident that implementation of our improvement plan will be a collaborative effort. I have strategies in place to ensure that we all feel responsible for seeing our improvement plan through.	
4. I have shared the details of our improvement plan with the staff in my school. They understand why the plan is important and how we will work together to make it a reality.	
5. I have specific strategies and ideas in mind to help monitor the implementation of our improvement plan.	
6. I am prepared to make adjustments as needed to ensure that our improvement plan is a success. I understand that this can be a messy process and may involve some trial and error.	
7. I know it is my job to evaluate our improvement plan using new data and begin the cycle of inquiry and improvement again.	
8. I plan on revisiting our value-added information next year to evaluate how our changes affected student growth.	

When you're finished, choose the two statements that gave you the most pause, and discuss them with a trusted colleague or a member of your leadership team.

Afterword

Nearly 300 years ago, on October 22, 1707, just off the southwestern tip of England, 4 homebound British ships ran aground, and 2,000 men lost their lives. There was no battle. The admiral miscalculated his position in the Atlantic Ocean, and his flagship smashed into the rocks off the coast of England. The rest of the fleet, following blindly behind, also went aground and piled up.

The concept of latitude and longitude had been around for a long time, but even as late as 1700, mariners had not managed to devise an accurate way to measure longitude. Nobody ever knew for sure how far east or west they had travelled. And that day when the fog was dense, the results were tragic.

In response, the British government created a competition to be judged by the Board of Longitude, offering a prize of $1 million (in today's dollars) to solve this measurement problem. Most expected the answer to come from the astronomers or scientists of the day. However, an English clockmaker, John Harrison, who pioneered the science of a portable, precision time-keeping device (chronometer) solved the problem. Yet, for the longest time, the Board of Longitude just wouldn't welcome a mechanical answer to what they saw as an astronomical question.

And likewise today, many educators still don't see the value of statistical answers to education challenges. Value-added analysis has shown itself to be, in part, a statistical answer to our quest to improve student achievement. As seafarers needed accurate readings of latitude and longitude, today's educators need readings of both progress and achievement to determine direction and destination of students. It's not the exclusiveness of *or* but the brilliance of *and*. We need both.

Today's modern computing power, coupled with data from student achievement testing, provides us a wealth of information that, when properly mined, can assist us in making wise choices with respect to instructional practices and programs. Taking a page from arguments made about guns: data doesn't change practice, people do. You can see from the numerous examples provided herein that value-added analysis provides a lens that truly provides evidence to lever changes that benefit students. It affirms empirically what all students have known forever: great teachers matter.

Purpose of Value-Added Analysis

Our work with value-added reporting has never been simply to prove but rather to improve. In this book, we've highlighted a multi-step process with value-added data at the center that can help principals and teachers share practices, look for relationships, and develop strategies to improve student achievement. We've also seen how a child's zip code may define where they are but not where they are going. Why would a teacher who has a disproportionate number of poor or low-performing children want to continue teaching there if awards and recognition are limited to achievement? Value-added analysis levels the playing field by answering "What did you do with the children you taught?" rather than "Who did you get?" This is a twenty-first century tool that enables analysis of productivity.

Future of Value-Added Analysis

Is value-added analysis a trend that we are likely to see come and go, vis-à-vis modern mathematics, site-based management, or the overhead projector? That's not likely given the value of the information it provides to make key decisions. The danger, of course, lies in overreaching its capacity to discern, almost single-handedly, good teaching. The danger will come in the form of leadership that uses this data as a single weapon of judgment as opposed to a complementary instrument of learning.

Here's a practical example. A speaker meeting with a large group of reformers recently asked, "How many of you believe we can take something as complex as the development of human intellectual capital in children, assess it with an annual test, parse out the appropriate teacher attribution, and then pay, hire, and fire teachers on that basis?" The answer from the group was overwhelmingly affirmative because of our need to quickly determine accountability or assign blame. It's so much easier if you can distill something down to a simple number from 1 to 10 that everyone can understand. However, it is a disservice to the complexity of teaching to ever believe it can really be that simple—because it isn't.

Can value-added analysis contribute answers to the questions of accountability, compensation, and evaluation? Absolutely! It's a misnomer to make it the sole piece for any of those or, frankly, for any improvement. Just as pictures are improved through the use of more pixel points, so is our assessment of instruction enhanced by multiple data points.

At this writing, Race to the Top, with one of its four assurances focused squarely on effective teachers and leaders, would appear to make value-added analysis a critical piece of evidence on the efficacy of our work. Merit pay of the 1980s, and even career ladders, often went by the wayside because of the appearance of only subjective data. The Bill and Melinda Gates Foundation is using their Measures of Effective Teaching Project to help discern those factors that contribute most to student learning. They are doing it empirically, and value-added calculations are serving as a rich source of evidence and independent data. They are asking questions such as, Is there a relationship between how students view teachers and academic gain? They are using digital panoramic cameras to capture classroom performance to answer the question, What are teachers doing to produce gains?

We believe that the continuous improvement approach emphasized in this book will enable value-added analysis to be used by educators to improve effectiveness. At its best, the goals of value-added analysis ought to be assisting the *uncovering, discovering, and recovering* and not simply the *naming, blaming and, shaming*. That, of course, leads to a critical piece of all reform efforts and tools, including this one—leadership.

Leadership

Just as great teaching matters for students, so does great leading. It becomes impossible to create the improvement culture we have discussed without effective leadership. Does it have to be the principals? After all, they are the ones who decide which data will be used, assign time for collaboration or not, develop teams or not, and assign inquiry or blame. The school culture is largely influenced by the principal. It becomes too hard and unsustainable for a group of well-intentioned, reform-minded teachers to work around the principal. What works best, of course, is collaboration between the leader, teachers, and other stakeholders to improve student achievement.

At the heart of the leader's responsibility is the need to inspire trust, especially around the use of data. We have found leaders who can lead and inspire crucial conversations around improvement. They create an atmosphere of trust and inquiry and use data that supports actions that create extraordinary student results. These are leaders who focus on strengths first but also facilitate discussions or implement actions that cause things to happen with people and for children. It is hard to overstate the importance of leadership in creating and instilling a culture that empowers, offers hope, discusses, and acts on behalf of children.

Improving Effective Teaching

Our work with districts has enabled us to identify teachers who consistently make huge student gains each year with different groups of students. Repeated conversations and interviews with these teachers using appreciative inquiry strategies have yielded several revelations. One is that great teaching is not made out of a half dozen unitary actions that can be written, easily described, and, if implemented, will improve student achievement. Student learning is not the enemy of enthusiasm, passion, or a consequence of those who try to ensure that students properly answer every last multiple-choice question. Indeed, what we have discovered is that effective teachers are able to build relationships with students, expect productivity, and have classrooms with management structures to maintain discipline, while knowing when to be flexible enough for teachable moments. Great teaching appears to be a series of moves over time that make the movie as opposed to individual still shots. It's a process.

Do students work harder for someone they perceive actually cares for them enough to build relationships? Of course they do. The challenge for teachers is always when this is not balanced with the other pieces necessary to good teaching. For example, not expecting productivity at all is akin to really caring for someone except, of course, for their learning. On the other hand, focusing rigidly on productivity can create a sweatshop where students give up. Highly effective teachers take explicit, replicable steps to create environments that produce great learning results for students.

Can other teachers learn from them? Of course they can. One of the most powerful uses of value-added analysis is to use it along with other evidence to identify excellent teachers and learn from them. In fact, there is greater variance of teacher effectiveness across buildings than across districts. There are great teachers everywhere, and the key is identifying them, providing opportunities to learn from them, and leveraging their talent to help others. Their work fits perfectly into the seven-step systemic framework for improvement described throughout this book. These are the individuals who can help others think critically using the fishbone to clarify specific root causes and practices for improvement.

We'd like to end with one last story about a particular professor known for his high expectations of student work. The story goes that when you turn in a first draft of your paper, you get it back with instructions to simplify and clarify. A second iteration elicits the same instructions. It is only when the student turns the paper in for the fourth time that he finally agrees to read it for the first time!

The point here is that improvement is a process. Our step-by-step framework enables educators to systematically uncover evidence, ask questions, make assumptions, construct theories, design actions, and do it repeatedly to help students. The room for improvement is an ever-expanding one that becomes better when educators act upon the best evidence available.

Glossary

Above expected gain: Classification of performance assigned to a teacher, a school, or a district that is producing growth significantly above expected levels.

Aggregate data: Data that are brought together to examine larger scale results. Building data may be aggregated together to produce district data.

Below expected gain: Classification of performance assigned to a teacher, a school, or a district that is producing growth significantly below expected levels.

Cohort: A group or division of people or items. An example of a cohort of students is a group of all students in a building at a particular grade level.

Disaggregate data: Data that are broken into smaller pieces to examine results associated with smaller subgroups. Grade level data may be disaggregated into teacher-level subgroups.

Growth standard: The standard for the amount of growth a student is expected to achieve in a given year.

Longitudinal data: Data collected and linked over time.

Normal curve equivalent (NCE): The NCE scale is an equal interval scale that ranges in scores from 1 to 99. This equal interval property makes it a favorable metric for manipulating group achievement performances across years.

Observed scores: Actual scores that students earn on a test.

Progress: Amount of growth students experience during one academic year.

School diagnostic report: Provides achievement subgroup comparisons of student progress organized by grade level and subject area. Report displays progress by prior-achievement. Reports also can be generated for user-selected adequate yearly progress (AYP) subgroups.

School effect or mean NCE gain: Average impact the school has on students' progress in a specific grade level and subject area.

School value-added report: Provides aggregate growth rates for students across the tested subject areas in the school. Report displays student progress by grade level and subject area.

Standard error: A statistic that establishes a level of certainty associated with the estimated mean gain. Generally speaking, the smaller the standard error, the more precise the estimate of the effect. Whenever student test data are used to produce a value-added effect, standard error accompanies the effect.

Value-added analysis: Statistical methodology used to measure student progress.

Value-added summary report: Provides grade level by grade level comparisons of student progress rates in all schools in the district.

References

Aaronson, D., Barrow, L., & Sander, L. (2007). Teachers and student achievement in the Chicago public high schools. *Journal of Labor Economics, 25*(1), 95–135.

Bill & Melinda Gates Foundation. (2009, July). Speech to the National Conference of State Legislatures. Retrieved from http://www.gatesfoundation.org/speeches-commentary/Pages/bill-gates-2009-conference-state-legislatures.aspx.

Boston Public Schools. (1998, March 9). High school restructuring. Boston: Author

Coleman, J. (1966). *Equality of educational opportunity study*. Ann Arbor, MI: Inter-university Consortium for Political and Social Research.

Doran, G.T. (1981). There's a SMART way to write management's goals and objectives. *Management Review, 70*(11), 33–36.

Downey, C. J., Steffy, B. E., English, F. W., Frase, L. E., & Poston, W. K. (2004). *The three-minute classroom walk-through: Changing school supervisory practice one teacher at a time.* Thousand Oaks, CA: Corwin.

Duncan, A. (2009, July 24). Education reform's moon shot. *The Washington Post*. Retrieved from http://www.washingtonpost.com/wp-dyn/content/article/2009/07/23/AR2009072302634.html.

Felch, J., Song, J., & Smith, D. (2010, August 14). Who's teaching L.A.'s kids? *Los Angeles Times.* Retrieved from http://articles.latimes.com/2010/aug/14/local/la-me-teachers-value-20100815

Harris, D. N. (2011). *Value-added measures in education: What every educator needs to know.* Cambridge, MA: Harvard Education Press.

Hattie, J. (2009). *Visible learning.* London: Routledge, UK.

Haycock, K., & Crawford, C. (2008, April). Closing the Teacher Quality Gap. Educational Leadership, *65*(7), 14–19. Retrieved from http://www.ascd.org/publications/educational–leadership/apr08/vol65/num07/Closing-the-Teacher-Quality-Gap.aspx

Hershberg, T. (2004). *Value-added assessment: Powerful diagnostics to improve instruction and promote student achievement.* Monograph presented at American Association of School Administrators Women Administrators Conference, Arlington, VA.

Hoff, D. J. (1999). Echoes of the Coleman report. *Education Week, 18*(28), 33.

Jacob, B. A., Lefgren, L., & Sims, D. (2008). *The persistence of teacher-induced learning gains* (NBER Working Paper No. 14065). Cambridge, MA: National Bureau of Economic Research.

Jordan, H., Mendro, R., & Weerasinghe, D. (1997). *Teacher effects on longitudinal student achievement.* Dallas, TX: Dallas Independent School District.

Kane, T. J., & Staiger, D. O. (2008). *Estimating teacher impacts on student achievement: An experimental evaluation* (Preliminary draft PDF, NBER Working Paper No. 14607). Cambridge, MA: National Bureau of Economic Research.

Konstantopoulos, S. (2007). *How long do teacher effects persist?* (Discussion Paper No. 2893). Boston, MA: Boston College, Institute for the Study of Labor.

Marzano, R. J. (2000). *A new era in school reform: Going where the research takes us.* Aurora, CO: Mid-Continent Regional Education Lab.

McCaffrey, D. F., & Hamilton, L. S. (2007). *Value-added assessment in practice: Lessons from the Pennsylvania Value-Added Assessment System pilot project.* Santa Monica, CA: RAND.

National Commission on Excellence in Education. (1983). *A nation at risk: The imperative for educational reform.* Washington, DC: U.S. Government Printing Office.

Reeves, D. (2002). [Diagram]. *The leadership for learning framework.* Retrieved from http://www.ascd.org/publications/books/105151/chapters/Introduction@-What-The-Learning-Leader-Will-Do-for-You.aspx

Rivers, J. C. (2000). *The impact of teacher effect on student math competency achievement* (Doctoral dissertation, University Microfilms International, 9959317). Ann Arbor, MI: University of Tennessee.

Rivkin, S. G., Hanushek, E. A., & Kain, J. F. (2001). *Teachers, schools, and academic achievement* (Working Paper No. 6691, revised). Cambridge, MA: National Bureau of Economic Research

Rivkin, S. G., Hanushek, E. A., & Kain, J. F. (2005). Teachers, schools, and academic achievement. *Econometrica, 73*(2): 417–458.

Rockoff, J. E. (2004). The impact of individual teachers on student achievement: Evidence from panel data. *American Economic Review, 94*(2): 247–252.

Rossiter, M. (2002). *Narrative and stories in adult teaching and learning.* (ERIC Document Reproduction Service No. ED473147). Retrieved from ERIC database: http://www.eric.ed.gov/ERICWebPortal/custom/portlets/recordDetails/detailmini.jsp?_nfpb=true&_&ERICExtSearch_SearchValue_0=ED473147&ERICExtSearch_SearchType_0=no&accno=ED473147

Sanders, W. L. (2004, June). *A summary of conclusions drawn from longitudinal analysis of student achievement data over the past 22 years.* Paper presented to Governors Education Symposium, Asheville, NC.

Sanders, W. L., & Rivers, J. C. (2009). Choosing a value-added model. In T. Hershberg & C. Robertson-Kraft (Eds.), *A grand bargain for education reform: New rewards and supports for accountability* (pp. 43–58). Cambridge, MA: Harvard Education Press.

U.S. Department of Education. (2009). *Race to the top program executive summary* (CFDA number: 84.395). Retrieved from http://www.ed.gov/programs/racetothetop/index.html

University of Tennessee Value-Added Research and Assessment Center. (1997). *Graphical summary of educational findings from the Tennessee Value-Added Assessment System.* Knoxville: University of Tennessee.

Index

CORWIN
A SAGE Company

The Corwin logo—a raven striding across an open book—represents the union of courage and learning. Corwin is committed to improving education for all learners by publishing books and other professional development resources for those serving the field of PreK–12 education. By providing practical, hands-on materials, Corwin continues to carry out the promise of its motto: **"Helping Educators Do Their Work Better."**